NEVER ENOUGH

Separating Self-Worth from Approval

LEARN HOW TO BLOOM

from your inner wisdom and strength

&

feel the universe supporting you as you do!

Deb Lang, Psy.D.

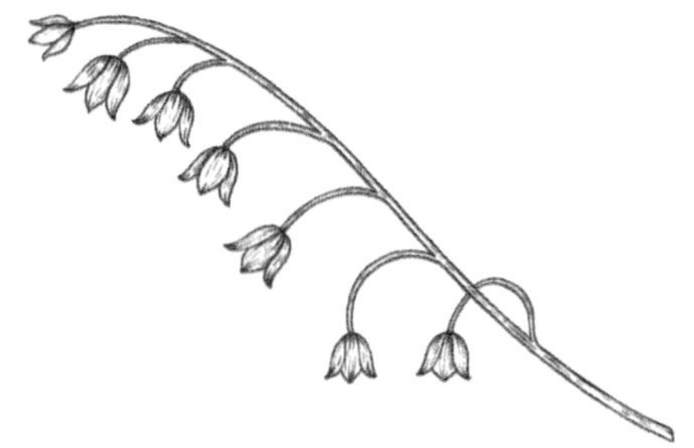

praise for *Never Enough*

"It was phenomenal."
It really helped me to feel seen and known."

Ellaine Kiel, early reader

"Never Enough is amazing! I learned so much from the
BLOOM model and have already experienced success
using it. I took notes for myself the whole way. I believe
ANYONE who reads this book will benefit as it is very
easy to understand and has a review in each chapter
for readers to see the info again."

Ginger Phillips, early reader

I loved this book! It's beautiful—warm, accepting,
hopeful and inspiring. Deb's writing is so intimate and
kind—smart and not intimidating. I am looking forward
to using this book with so many of my clients as these

*tools and practices are universally helpful. This book will
be a useful support in healing issues of self-worth,
self-compassion, and the ability to be authentic
and get one's needs met in relationships.*

Judy Zehr, (she/her) MHRM, LPC, early reader

*"This book is GREAT! Thank you for writing it.
I took lots of notes. It's the first time I feel like I'm
reading about myself with the guidance to make changes.
I will certainly be ordering extra copies to share
with my girlfriends!"*

Laura Stansberry,
Retired Banking Executive, early reader

*"While reading the first chapters of this book I was
surprised to find that I felt like it was written about my
life. The connection was so deep that I was motivated to
continue reading because of my strong desire to make
healthy changes in myself. I wish I would have had this
book earlier in my life! I can't wait to take
the companion course."*

Leigh Anne Francway, early reader

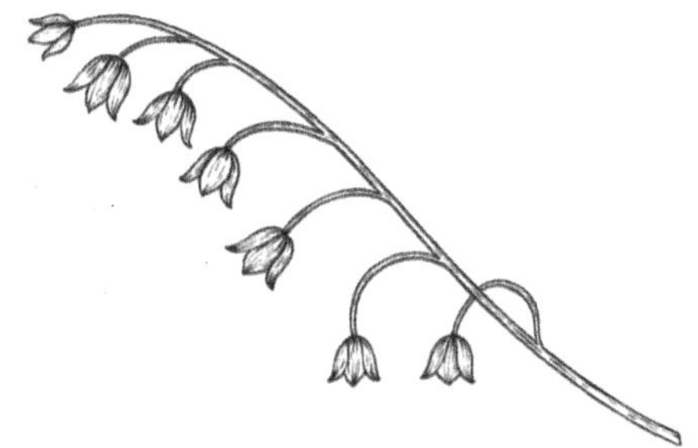

a gift for my readers

In part two of the book, you will learn how to tap into the treasure chest of wisdom that is right inside you. The first step in doing that is learning how to relax and create the space to connect with yourself.

First steps are usually a bit daunting, and I want to make getting started as easy as possible for you. My clients often find it helpful, in the beginning, to be guided as they practice the skills in this book.

So, to help you get started, I created a recording of me guiding you in this first step. With the recording you can simply relax and listen rather than continually referring to the book. You can also carry it with you and use it in times of need.

Download it here: bit.ly/Debsgifts4u

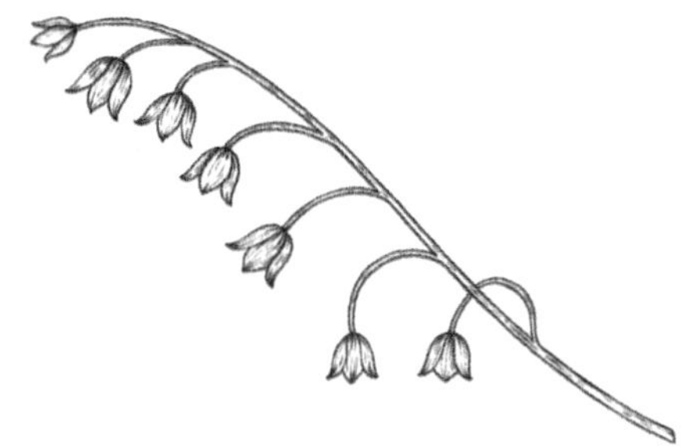

dedication

This book is dedicated to all women who believe they are "not enough." May you discover how very much is possible when you start loving, accepting, and trusting yourself.

contents

part two
the BLOOM model

part three
what your journey might look like

welcome

- Do you dream of feeling confident in your own skin?

- Of not spending your day worrying what people think and whether they will approve of you?

- Are you exhausted from trying to keep others happy or from saying "yes" when you really wanted to say "no?"

- Or can your day turn on a dime with a look or a comment?

- Has all of that left you feeling overwhelmed, anxious, or depressed?

- Maybe turning to food for comfort or wondering what is wrong with you?

It's not an easy way to walk through life, is it? I know because I've been there. And, as a licensed psychologist, I've worked with many women sharing similar struggles—smart, creative, capable women feeling stuck, overwhelmed, anxious, or depressed.

Many didn't realize their worth was tied to the approval of others—they simply felt a strong pull to do more or to be more. They couldn't find peace no matter how hard they tried. There always seemed to be one more thing they needed to work on or get done before they could relax.

Some knew the opinions of others were derailing them, and they couldn't break this pattern—leaving them feeling weak, guilty, or ashamed. Most were baffled by how they could be so good at caring for others yet find it so hard to do the same for themselves. Despite what you may think, I doubt you are weak, disorganized, or lack willpower. There are strong pulls—both internally and externally—keeping women looking outside of themselves for approval, while at the same time disconnecting them from their true selves and their internal wisdom.

Being appealing and chosen was once essential for our survival as women. Despite increased freedoms, how well we please others continues to be a measure of a woman's success, and these messages are reinforced in subtle and not so subtle ways. From childhood we are socialized to please, caretake, and to stay within the lines of what is socially acceptable. These messages are internalized and become well-traveled pathways in the brain.

These brain pathways become an internal force, pulling us to look outside of ourselves for safety and approval. They influence thoughts, feelings, and beliefs, as well as behaviors. They can leave you feeling vulnerable to forces from the outside, like the state of the world, societal norms, or big industries like the diet and fashion.

With the advent of social media, messages about who and how we should be are constant and the possibilities for comparison endless. And today, looking outside for safety and approval leaves women feeling vulnerable and insecure because "outside" doesn't feel very safe.

The interplay of these feelings of vulnerability, our wiring and societal pressures leave many, if not most, women constantly striving and never feeling as though they are secure, measure up, or are good enough.

The women who came to see me believed these struggles defined them. They didn't realize that instead, these patterns simply reflected well-traveled circuits or "wiring" in the brain. It is important to separate who we are from what we have wired in our brains.

These well-traveled circuits don't define you. They are simply patterns of behaviors, thoughts, and feelings that have become like highways in your brain.

The good news is that we now know the brain is constantly changing based on what we think, feel, and do. It was once believed that when we reached adulthood our brain was fixed or unchangeable. We now know that it is possible to change the structure of our brain. This is called neuroplasticity. When we purposely change our behaviors or reactions with enough regularity to change the pathways in our brain, this is called self-directed neuroplasticity.

We have likely barely scratched the surface of possibility when it comes to using our mind to change the brain or body. As advances in technology allow us to see what is happening in the brain in real time, we are learning more and more about how our behaviors, thoughts, feelings, and even our imagination change the brain.

To give you an example of the power of the mind to change the brain, let me share with you a study comparing the effects on the brain of imagined piano practice with actual practice.

In her book *Train your Mind Change Your Brain*, Sharon Begley shares a study by Pascual-Leone in which he had a group of volunteers merely think about practicing the piano.[1] They played the piano piece in their heads—imagining their fingers moving over the keys, while never actually touching a piano. Results of the study showed that mental rehearsal expanded the regions of the brain controlling finger movement just as it did in those who actually played the piano.

I am amazed when I read the many studies like this. I'm hoping you feel excited and hopeful as well. Even if you aren't ready to face disapproval in real life, you can begin working on your reactions in the safety of your imagination.

Learning about the brain and how it pulls us to do what we have done before, especially if this is related to safety, has helped my clients let go of shame and blame. It has helped them to realize that they aren't weak or defective—instead they simply have wiring that is defective or unreasonable that needs updating.

My desire to help more women let go of shame and blame was the major motivator in my deciding to write this book. I'd like to help you step out of the no-win struggle of basing your worth on the reactions of others, because

you deserve to be you even if others disagree!

My gift, as a psychologist, is helping women connect with their own wisdom and strength. I'd like to help you connect with the treasure chest of strength, wisdom, and power that is waiting right there inside of you. You may not believe that it is there, and it is. It is just being overrun by a strong pull for approval or other outdated faulty assumptions about yourself.

In this book we will look at both the external forces and the internal wiring that keeps women looking outside of themselves for the measure of their worth. And I will share with you, information, tools, and a plan to help you bring new information into old faulty wiring, as well as to tap into your inner treasure chest.

My vision for you and for all women is a move from the outdated pull to find safety through approval to a place grounded on the firm foundation of your own wisdom—feeling safe to be yourself, to support and be supported by other women, and to feel supported by larger sources of support like the spiritual. I want you to have the chance to bloom and blossom in the magnificent way that is only possible for you.

Just as a daffodil bulb is destined to be a daffodil and not a tulip, you are destined to be who you were meant to be, not what someone else wants you to be. No matter how much a daffodil might be told they should be more like a tulip, a daffodil is going to be a daffodil.

If I am disappointed with the daffodil because it's not a tulip and don't take care of it, it's still going to be a daffodil, and it won't be the healthy, gorgeous daffodil it might be with loving care.

In the same way, striving to be what you think others want you to be can lead you away from your own self-care and prevent you from blossoming into all that you could and are meant to be. So, let's look at the forces linking worth and approval and talk about how you can start bringing new information into this old wiring which has connected your self-worth with the approval of others.

With much love and support for your blossoming and blooming—in whatever form that takes,

a few things before we start

information vs prescription

I am sharing this information with you for informational and educational purposes only. I am not diagnosing or prescribing what you should do. I am sharing general information in the form of a self-help tool for your own use. It is up to you to determine the degree of risk there will be for you in taking this course.

Taking this course does not mean that I am your therapist. The information I share is not meant to replace the advice of any of your health care providers. In offering this self-help tool, I am making no guarantees regarding the effectiveness of the information that I share.

my perspective

Never Enough is written from the perspective of a cisgender white woman of privilege from the American West. I am not assuming to know or understand the experience of all women. I recognize that your experience may differ from mine, even if you too grew up in the

United States and that the experience of women of different races, cultures or sexual orientations may not have followed the same trajectory as I describe in chapter two. As I look back on our history as women, I am doing so based on my knowledge and experience of a heterosexual, patriarchal society.

I do imagine that the experiences of all the women around the world are felt by each of us through the collective female consciousness. And I hope that wherever you are, and despite our differences, you will find the skills of the BLOOM model useful. I would love to learn from your experiences and reactions. You can share those with me at info@creatingchoicesdeblang.com.

client stories

I knew that sharing client experiences would be helpful in writing this book because women often feel alone when dealing with these issues. I struggled with how to do that while maintaining my client's privacy and my duty to maintain confidentiality. To accomplish both goals, I created individual clients from a compilation of the experiences of my clients over the years. When I did mention something unique to a particular client, I changed identifying information. In this way, you as the reader will have the opportunity to see how these patterns or struggles with approval played out in the lives of women and the kinds of changes that are possible.

If you are a client of mine and see yourself in the stories or words that I share, I hope that doing so will help you realize that you were not alone in these struggles and experiences—that there were many women over the years facing similar situations and having nearly identical responses.

repetition

As you are reading, you may notice that I repeat information and concepts throughout the book. I have done this purposely knowing from my experience that repetition is important in reinforcing new ways of thinking. This is especially true when the information contradicts your current beliefs or wiring. So many of my clients have said, "You have said this so many times, and this is the first time it made sense to me." Ideas and skills often just don't make sense until we are ready for them.

"and" versus "but"

The other thing you may notice in reading the book is my avoidance of the word "but" or other variations of that word. My editor and proofreader struggled with this, so I'm imagining you may as well.

I did this to encourage "both/and" thinking which is important in changing wires related to worth. In changing these wires, we are striving for inclusion. Others are entitled to their opinion, *and* you to yours. Others may disagree *and* your opinion still has value. For instance, "You may not like my career choice, *and* I know that it is right for me." If I can accept both, I can be myself and maintain connection.

The goal is to be able to hold both. In a sentence with the word "but," the "but" negates the first half of the sentence. Think of a time when someone starts a sentence, and you can tell by their tone that a "but" is coming. It is hard to believe what comes before the "but," isn't it?

For women with, this style of relating the use of the word "but" often shows up in disconnecting, a pattern you will learn about in the book, and one I suspect you will relate to. The goal in this work is to get to the place where there is an acceptance of both—others can have their feelings, *and* you can have yours.

companion workbook

At the end of each chapter, I provide a summary of the main points in the chapter, in a section I've named, "in a nutshell." I also offer questions to stimulate your thinking about how the information in the chapters shows up or impacts your own life. These questions can be found in the "ideas for reflection" section at the end of each chapter. My clients often find it helpful to take notes during or after our sessions, and then later reflect on what they have written. The act of writing and then reading what we have written is useful, as it engages different parts of the brain.

I know for me it is easy to get caught up in reading a book and not really stop to reflect on what I am reading, or I might jot down notes on a piece of paper—never to be found again.

There is certainly nothing wrong with simply reading the book for informational purposes. I hope you enjoy it. And if you want to work on changing the wiring linking your worth with the approval of others, you will have the best chance of doing so by stopping to reflect and by applying the information and skills to your own life.

To help you with that, and to help you avoid the frustration of looking for random pieces of paper with notes you hoped to hold on to, I created a workbook for you with the ideas for reflection from each chapter. There is space there for you to jot down notes, reflect, or do some drawing.

This companion workbook for *Never Enough* is specifically designed to accompany the book and is available for purchase separately.

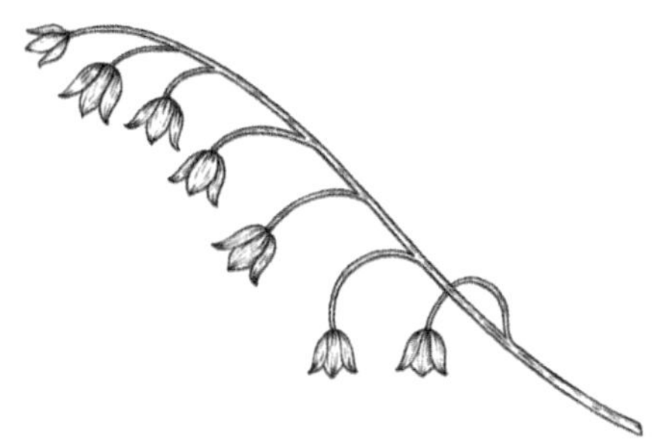

part one

why approval?

chapter one
you try so hard

Margaret*, a new client, oozed kindness. She smiled and thanked me for getting her in. She was easy to be around, and I had the sense I would enjoy working with her. Here's what Margaret had to say.

"I'm here because I've been feeling stressed and anxious and maybe depressed. It seems that no matter how hard I try, something isn't going right. Someone in the family has a problem I need to fix, or someone is unhappy for some reason or another. I have two teenagers and between trying to keep things goings smoothly at home and at work, I think it's getting to me. I'm worried about my blood pressure, and as you can see, I struggle with my weight. I am worried. I'm going to get diabetes. And I know my husband liked me

---

*   The narratives I provide are compilations of my client's experience and my words remembering their voices to ensure confidentiality. When I did mention something unique to a client, I changed identifying information. I have also used a different font to help you "hear" their voices, as well as mine whenever I share my voice.

better when I was thinner. He doesn't say anything, and I can tell by the way he looks at me. I've tried every diet there is and just can't seem to stick to it. He has heart disease and diabetes, so it bothers me that I don't do a better job of keeping things running smoothly at home, and I guess I do worry he will leave me. I really don't know what my problem is whether I'm just unorganized, or maybe I have problems with attention. I worry I might be getting some kind of early dementia. I've read books and searched online for how to keep a household running smoothly with teenagers. Nothing seems to help. I just can't seem to stay on top of things. What is wrong with me that I can't keep up?"

When I asked Margaret what she wished for herself, she replied:

"To feel on top of things. To feel like I have done enough so that I can relax and do the things I never get the chance to do."

Margaret's frustrations have been shared by so many women who have come for help—feeling like what they did wasn't enough. Not:

- organized enough
- calm enough
- thin enough
- self-controlled enough
- popular enough
- active enough

I could keep going, and I think you get the idea. I'm wondering if you relate. Does it seem like no matter how hard you try, it's not enough? That you're not enough? That you don't measure up? That you can't relax?

I bet, like Margaret, it's not for a lack of trying. I imagine you work really hard to stay on top of things and to feel secure that you've "done enough." I'm guessing you are an intelligent, intuitive woman, and it drives you crazy that you haven't been able to figure out why you can't get to the calm and secure place you are hoping for. As a result, you may be feeling overwhelmed, anxious, or depressed. Or your health may be suffering.

I'm writing this book because so many of my female clients discovered they had been working hard to solve problems that weren't the real problem. Like Margaret, many were trying to get more organized or lose weight. Others came in viewing anxiety or depression as the problem to be solved.

They were focusing on symptoms rather than the larger problem. Because of this, they were spinning their wheels. And the more you spin your wheels not getting anywhere, the more it chips away at your mood, confidence, and health.

Since you never seem to get there, you keep thinking the problem is you; it keeps you wondering:

- "What's wrong with me?"
- "Why can other people be organized, stay on top of things, and lose weight, and I can't?"
- "Why can't I get to the place where I can relax?"
- "What must people think of me?"

And because you believe the problem is with you, nothing in your life may feel very secure. Not relationships. Not your job. And the slightest hint of disapproval confirms your worries.

A man you recently started dating hasn't called you all weekend, and you worry that he is no longer interested or has moved on.

Your boss hasn't been as talkative and friendly as usual, and your anxiety spikes. Your thoughts drift to, "Maybe she's unhappy with me."

Your husband arrives home from work, takes one look at the house, and your heart sinks. You look around, feeling guilty that you haven't done the cleaning you had planned to do.

Peace and security continually elude you. It never ends, and it's never enough. No matter how hard you try, you can't seem to reach that place where you feel secure.

Over the years, I've listened to so many loving, intelligent, capable women feeling as if what they do is never enough and experiencing so much anguish as a result.

the pattern

As I listened to all this pain and struggle, I noticed a pattern. A pattern of relating to others that was showing up in many of the women who came to see me.

I started sharing this pattern with my clients, and their reaction was huge. It stopped them in their tracks. I heard things like,

"Oh my gosh, you are describing me exactly," Or, "This is under everything."

Sharing this pattern generated some of the biggest ah-ha moments in my work with these women. It made a difference in their lives, and they have consistently wanted to learn more.

I hope this book will help you explore whether this pattern is "alive and well" in your life.

what you can expect

Many books make big promises. I won't do that. Here's what I hope will happen.

I hope you'll discover that this feeling of "never being enough" isn't about you: that you are not defective, don't have problems with attention, aren't getting dementia, and that if you are turning to food for comfort, there's a good reason. I hope you will realize that this isn't personal—instead there are strong forces pulling you to look outside of yourself for validation of your worth.

Next, I hope you will begin to connect with yourself using the skills of the BLOOM model. By doing that you will start to bring new information into the outdated default wiring linking your worth with the approval of others. As you bring new information into these old faulty wires, I hope you will feel the freedom to bloom into the most radiant version of yourself.

our journey

In part one, we'll explore the forces and pressures that keep women looking outside of themselves for approval. We'll consider the history and experience of women and how our safety as women has been linked with approval—making it difficult to change.

I'll introduce you to the pattern I repeatedly noticed in women struggling to feel "enough" and that I came to call an entangled intimacy style. To help you get a sense of this style of relating, I'll share some of my experiences, as well as the experiences of some of my clients. We'll also talk about the ways this pattern may be impacting your life and creating struggles for you.

In part two, we'll move on to what I am imagining is your biggest question—"How can I change this?" Because knowledge is rarely enough to make these types of significant changes, I will introduce you to the "BLOOM" model.

This model will teach you how you can begin "rewiring" the core assumptions of this pattern that have most likely become the defaults or the automatic pathways in your brain for interacting with others. You will learn how to be there for yourself in a way that will help you deal with disapproval and tap into your own wisdom and strength.

I imagine you may immediately skip ahead to that section. I probably would as well. No worries if you do. Take a peek. Start practicing. There's no harm in doing so.

After you do, I encourage you to come back and keep reading. Most people find that understanding the pattern makes changing it much easier. Understanding the core beliefs of this pattern will help you notice them when they are operating rather than simply being caught up in them. Awareness is the first step in change.

In part three, I share some changes my clients have experienced in their lives by addressing this pattern, as well as obstacles you may encounter in working on this pattern in your own life. I'll also share my hopes for you.

you know yourself better than I do

This seems like a good time to remind you that this book is written to be educational and informative rather than as a prescription for what you should do. It is not intended to replace the advice of your health care provider(s). My providing you with this information does not mean that we have a therapist/client relationship. If something I say doesn't feel right for you, trust your gut and check with your own therapist or health care provider.

It is also quite possible that as you explore these patterns, feelings and memories will come up. If you feel overwhelmed by feelings, especially if you have a history of trauma, please reach out and get some support from your therapist or a therapist in your area.

Finally, in case you are wondering whether you will have wasted your money on this book if it turns out you don't have this style of relating, the answer to that question is a resounding "no."

The BLOOM model I will introduce you to can be useful for anyone feeling stressed, anxious, or depressed, or for anyone who wants to learn how to tap into their inner wisdom and strength. The learning you will be doing about rewiring default beliefs can be applied to any automatic unreasonable assumptions you might want to change.

All right let's dive in and start talking about this pattern that may be keeping you looking outside of yourself for approval.

in a nutshell

- If you are reading this book, I imagine you are an intelligent, intuitive woman who has been working hard to feel "good enough" and to get to the calm and secure place of your dreams.

- Because you try so hard and never seem to get there, you may be feeling overwhelmed, anxious, or depressed, or your health may be suffering.

- So many of my female clients discovered they had been working hard to solve problems that weren't the real problem.

- They were focusing on symptoms rather than the larger problem. Because of this, they were spinning their wheels and believing the problem was with them—that they were defective in some way.

- As I listened to women over the years, I noticed a pattern of relating to others that was showing up in so many of the women who came to see me.

- Sharing this pattern with women generated some of the biggest "ah-ha" moments in my work with women and led to big changes in their lives.

- I hope that you will learn, as they did, that you are not the problem. There are strong forces both externally and internally pulling you to look outside of yourself for your sense of worth.

- In part one we will look at those forces, as well as the pattern of relating that reinforces this tendency to look outside for approval.

- Then in part two you will learn strategies for changing these patterns through the BLOOM model.

- This model will teach you how you can begin "rewiring" the core assumptions of this pattern that have most likely become the defaults or the automatic pathways in your brain for interacting with others.

- And as you bring new information into old wires, I hope you will feel the freedom to bloom into the most radiant version of yourself.

ideas for reflection

- In what ways do you work hard to be "enough?"

- What impact has the striving you have been doing to be good enough had on you, both emotionally and physically?

- In what ways have you blamed yourself for looking outside yourself for approval?

chapter two
the invisible pull for approval

*"To totally accept the cultural definitions of femininity and
conform to the pressures is to kill the self."*

Mary Pipher, Ph.D.[2]

In this chapter we will look more closely at the entangled intimacy style and why it may be so common in women. To do that we'll consider our history as women and the strong societal pressures pushing us to look outside of ourselves for our value, while simultaneously abandoning our true selves.

This is a long chapter, and so I have broken it into parts to give you the opportunity to stop and reflect on what you have read. Let's start by looking more closely at the pattern I noticed in the women coming to see me.

chapter two
part one

I'm okay if you're okay

As I shared with you in the last chapter, over the years in working with women, I noticed a pattern. Women were using very similar words to describe a powerful pull to keep others happy, avoid disapproval, keep the peace, and "stay within the lines" of what is acceptable, all while ignoring their own needs.

I came to think of this pattern as an invisible force because most women were, initially, unaware of its power. These beliefs were unconscious and so much a part of what *felt* normal that most women weren't aware of them. Without their awareness, this force was keeping women linking their self-worth with the approval of others and leaving them feeling as though they were never enough.

It was resulting in constant striving and leading to the symptoms that were bringing many women in to see me. Whether it was exhaustion, overwhelm, anxiety, depression, or overeating, the pull to look outside oneself for worth kept showing up.

what the pattern looks like

The following beliefs drive an entangled intimacy style.

- "I need to keep you happy to know that I am okay and lovable."
- "If I don't keep you happy, or you disapprove of me, you

will leave me."

- "If I love you, I should 'intuit' your needs."
- "If I love you or care about you, I should feel the way you do about things," or "I should agree with you."

And because these beliefs define love, I expect the same in return.

- "If you love me, you should know what I need." "You should agree with me and my feelings."
- "If you don't intuit my needs, share similar feelings, or agree with me, you must not love me."

What is your reaction to reading these beliefs? Do they resonate or do they sound absurd?

I suspect that for most women, on the surface, these ideas sound ridiculous. Said out loud or reading them, they make little sense. For this reason, when women uncover these beliefs, they often feel embarrassed and wonder what is "wrong" with them for having such beliefs.

Similarly, theorists often describe these patterns in a way that suggests insufficiency. The pattern might be described as codependency[3] or a lack of maturity.[4]

Instead, my hunch is that this pattern reflects a style of relating which once kept women safe and which now is reinforced, or perhaps a better word is enforced, by cultural expectations, norms for women, and the interests of big industries.

This pattern of being what others expect seems, for many, to have morphed into a definition of what it means to love and be loved.

For women with this pattern, the core beliefs are an invisible force driving their interactions with other people and the world. Women simply feel the need to do more, be more, be "good enough," and often feel disappointed in relationships as the caring they give others is not reciprocated.

Let's spend a few minutes talking about how this pattern may have developed in the female experience and why it results in so much stress.

if I am cast out, I will die

Early in our history as humans, male or female, being accepted and included in our tribe was a matter of life and death. If we were cast out, death was inevitable.

Through the study of epigenetics, we now know the environment affects our genes and that these changes can pass from one generation to the next.[5] We also know that we carry the trauma of our ancestors in our genes.[6]

So, it seems likely that we all carry, in our genes, a fear of being rejected or "cast out" because of its connection with the risk of death. To avoid rejection, approval from others must have been necessary.

With time, it became possible to live independently. While men gained rights and freedoms, a woman's survival remained dependent on the decisions of others, often leaving women powerless in the face of marginalization, misogyny, and violence.

I share the following information about our history with one goal in mind. I hope that if you have been blaming yourself or feeling weak and defective because of this pattern, that reading about our history will help you let go of blaming and gain a better understanding of why so many women may struggle with these tendencies.

misogyny and marginalization

It would be another book for me to review all of the ways that women have been marginalized or have been victims of misogyny throughout our history. Jenny Holland's words, as she writes about her father in the forward of his book, *A Brief History of Misogyny: The World's Oldest Prejudice*, speaks to this. She writes,

> *"While he was writing he became consumed by the astonishing list of crimes committed against women by their husbands, fathers, neighbours and rulers. My mother and I would shudder as he recounted them..."*[7]

To make matters worse, for much of our history, we lacked any right to defend ourselves. In England and its colonies, it was widely believed that women were not intelligent or competent enough to appear in court or make business deals on their own. Women lived in what was called coverture, meaning women were under the legal and economic control of men. Before marriage, a woman's father made her decisions. After marriage, that right passed on to her husband.[8]

It wasn't until 1920 that in the United States, the 19th Amendment was passed, giving women the right to vote.[9] While this may seem like a long time ago to many of you reading this book, in reality, it was only a few generations ago. And, although we gained the right to vote, we have continued to be denied the same rights and privileges afforded to men. A conversation I had with a client this morning provides an example of this.

This morning during our session, my client, who is in her 70s, was feeling discouraged about her progress in therapy. She spoke of continuing fears about not being "enough" and feeling worried that there is more she "should do" or "be prepared for." Her discouragement had been triggered by comparisons with other women. She has, in fact, made more progress than she was recognizing in that moment.

We spent time talking about how common and predictable these struggles are for women and how difficult they can be to change. We thought about how valuable appeasing, avoiding disapproval as well as being constantly vigilant had been in the past for women in order to stay safe and get what they needed. As we talked, she began to feel less "defective." She also recalled a memory from childhood.

She shared that following her father's death, her mother went to the bank in hopes of securing a loan. She said that her parents weren't rich, and they were comfortable and well-known in the community. Despite having used this bank for years, her mother's application was denied based on her being a "single woman." My client recounted her mother's fear and anger.

She realized that by hearing her mother's experiences, she had internalized a fear of not being able to get what she needed, along with fear that she wouldn't be safe. These fears have become the lens through which she views life as an adult.

This example happened many years ago. And today, women continue to be treated unfairly and to encounter the message that it is unsafe to be themselves.

feeling unsafe to be yourself

There are many ways that women fear being themselves. We will talk more about this in part two of this chapter. One of the fears women have expressed to me is a fear of their emotionality. Although no longer diagnosed as "hysteria," many women fear how their emotionality will be judged. Or, in the words of so many clients,

"How can people see me as credible or competent when I cry?"

And then there is the fear of being seen as a "bitch" or a "whiney woman" if you need to stand your ground or complain. For female journalists who speak out, digital harassment is common. There have been threats of rape and death. It is often unending, frightening, and destructive to women's lives.[10]

Margaret Sullivan quoted Elisa Lees Muñoz, the executive director of the International Women's Media Foundation, who described this harassment as "clearly an effort to silence women's voices in public spaces."[11]

In an article in The Washington Post, Monica Hesse, a columnist on gender and its impact on society, writes, "Capitol rioters searched for Nancy Pelosi in a way that should make every woman's skin crawl."[12] She recounts rioters calling out, "Oh Naaaaaaancy" in a singsong voice which is right out of a scene in a horror movie. And it is not only women in the public eye who fear for their safety.

Domestic violence, sexual abuse, and rape are a reality for many women, and for many others, these worries are alive in their fears. I imagine many of you can think of a time when you felt unsafe or in danger from a man in your life or men around you. I certainly can.

And we continue to be treated unfairly. According to Christine Michel Carter, author and advocate for working moms, women continue to be marginalized in the workplace. She writes,

"Women are treated unfairly at work, no matter their age or race," and *"Laws and public opinion have changed significantly in the past 50 years, but women continue to lag behind their male counterparts in senior job titles and salaries. As of 2021, women made about 80 cents to the dollar a man made in a comparable job."*[13]

survival and an entangled intimacy style

Thinking about our history of marginalization, violence, and misogyny, wouldn't it make sense that women would use whatever means possible to survive? And wouldn't it be essential to be pleasing, chosen, and "good enough" in order to stay safe and have any chance of getting what one might need? Also necessary would be the skill of intuiting the needs and desires of those wielding power—a skill that is highly developed in those with this intimacy style.

In order to stay safe, this entangled style of relating must have become so well practiced, that it came to be seen as normal, right, and expected. And because of this it was passed, without questioning, from one generation to the next, even when women did gain more rights and freedoms.

In filmmaker Renata Keller's documentary, *Why Women Need to Climb Mountains—on a Journey through the Life and Vision* of *Dr. Gerda Lerner*, Dr. Lerner shares,

"We define what our goals are and what we think is possible to reach in our lives by the stories we inherit about the people who came before us and who are like us."[14]

early socialization

One way these stories have been conveyed is through our early socialization. Women are taught to be kind, to keep the peace, not to make waves, and to stay within the lines of what is acceptable. We are socialized to look pretty and to be chosen—to find a mate and become a mother. As Rebecca, a woman in her mid-60s shared with me, when she was learning to play tennis, her mother instructed her, when playing with boys, to "Play nice and don't play to win."

Socialization doesn't only happen in the home. Peers become a major influence, as does social media. Mary Pipher, Ph.D., a clinical psychologist with years of experience working with adolescent girls, shares in her book, *Reviving Ophelia: Saving the Lives of Adolescent Girls*, her fears of the "girl poisoning" culture that girls were growing up in during the 90s.[15]

It is frightening to think of how much worse these forces must be now in the time of social media. At that time, she described increasing levels of sexism and violence, the devaluing of female intelligence, and sexual harassment, even in elementary schools. The client stories she shares are both alarming and heartbreaking.

Pipher quotes Simone de Beauvoir as asserting, "Girls stop being and start seeming." Pipher then goes on to say,

"Vibrant, confident girls become shy, doubting young women.
Girls stop thinking, 'Who am I? What do I want?' and start
thinking, 'What must I do to please others?'"

I don't work with adolescents in my practice, and I see the impact of this learning in the women who come to see me. Many feel lost about who they are in the world or what they might need or want if they were to stop focusing so much on the needs of others. Most worry about the repercussions of being themselves.

an invisible force

Women's history scholar Alice Kessler-Harris, Ph.D., shares in the ColumbiaX online course, *Women Have Always Worked*, that when the history of women became a field of study, it was necessary to *"understand the mechanism that kept women in their places and convinced them that it was natural for their roles to be limited."*[16]

Throughout our history there have been numerous external forces limiting our roles and keeping us in our place. Our socialization to appease, be chosen and avoid disapproval seems to have become an internal force keeping us constantly striving, unable to relax, feel confident, trust our own wisdom, or feel safe to compete.

Most women are unaware of this deep connection between their worth and approval because it operates at an unconscious level. On the surface it looks as though we have moved beyond the barriers of the past. Women are encouraged to get an education and pursue a career. We can live independently and run for office. And yet, deep inside we worry about whether we are enough. We compare ourselves to others and most often feel lacking. It seems no matter how hard we try we can't get to the place where we can relax.

While it is no longer necessary to be appealing or chosen to survive, that learning is alive and well in our subconscious. Without our awareness, this entangled style of relating becomes a self-imposed prison with the potential to perpetuate injustice and put us at risk of losing our rights and privileges. If we do not change this pattern, we will remain captives—constantly striving for approval with our self-worth hanging in the balance.

Or as John Berger so aptly described it,

"A woman has to survey everything she is and does because how she appears to others is crucially important for what is normally thought of as the success of her life. Her sense of self is supplanted by a sense of being appreciated as herself by another."[17]

Or our sense of self is usurped by how much we feel others appreciate us. Being ourselves and the act of choosing gets lost in being appealing and chosen.

We look outside for how we "should" be, especially regarding our appearance. And as a result, we become victims of powerful fashion and dieting industries happy to dictate how we should look and dress.

Before we move on to talking about the interaction of these patterns with outside forces in regard to appearance, let's take a moment to reflect on what we have covered so far.

in a nutshell

- In an entangled intimacy style, self-worth and safety are linked with approval from others.

- I know that I am "good" and "okay" if I keep you happy. If I don't keep you happy, or you disapprove of me, I am not "okay," and you will abandon me.

- For many women, these beliefs seem to have morphed into what it means to love and be loved.

- Although these beliefs may sound absurd, they make sense in light of our history.

- Early in our history, to be cast out of the tribe meant certain death for both men and women. Over time, males gained more rights and freedoms, while for a great many years, women lacked these rights and remained dependent on males for their safety and survival.

- Women have been marginalized or victims of misogyny throughout our history and to make matters worse, for much of that time, we lacked the right to defend ourselves.

- Women lived in coverture, meaning they were under the legal and economic control of men.

- Despite gaining the right to vote in the United States in 1920, women have continued to be denied all the rights and privileges of men—being treated unfairly at work and earning less money for similar work.

- Being pleasing and "good enough," or having an entangled intimacy style, would have been essential to stay safe when women lacked legal rights. Also necessary would be the skill of intuiting the needs and desires of those in power—a skill which is highly developed in this intimacy style.

- Because of its necessity, an entangled style of relating must have become so well practiced in the lives of women that it came to be seen as normal and expected.

- And because it was expected, it was passed from one generation to the next without questioning, even when women gained more rights and freedoms.

- As a result our socialization to appease, be chosen and stay within the lines of what has been seen as acceptable became an internal force holding us captive and limiting our ability to relax, feel confident, trust our wisdom or compete.

- If we don't change this pattern, we may unknowingly perpetuate injustice and lose more rights and freedoms.

- Because we look outside of ourselves for how we "should" be and look, we become vulnerable to big industries like the media, fashion, and diet industries.

ideas for reflection

- What feelings came up as you read this section?
- In what ways were you socialized to please, look pretty, or keep the peace?
- In what ways have you been afraid to be yourself or felt fearful of speaking up because of being female?

chapter two
part two

appearance as the measuring stick

In the last section, we began exploring the forces driving women to look outside themselves for value and to be chosen. If a woman is to be chosen, she must first attract. Attracting might not be such a scary proposition if we were encouraged to be ourselves, no matter what our shape or size.

Instead, big businesses like the diet, fashion, and media, as well as social standards, dictate how we "should" look. Because of our socialization, women are eager to find out what is attractive, which opens the door for big industries to provide the answer.

We are constantly bombarded with images of these standards for beauty. And because there is very little variation in the ideals presented to us, women are led to believe there is only one way to be appealing.[18]

Hirschmann and Munter describe the result as "Bad Body Fever"—a social ill. These authors point to commercials using actresses and models with bodies unlike the typical woman and then on top of that having been retouched and airbrushed to achieve even a higher degree of perfection. The authors write that these ads convey a "dual message—buy this item" and, "If you look like me, people will notice you."[19]

And to make matters worse, styles and fashion are constantly changing, leaving women trying to keep up and be seen as acceptable in their appearance. The advent of the internet and social media has astronomically increased the opportunities to view these images and make comparisons.

Even though most of us know that the images we see in ads and the media have been altered, because we see them so often, the women we see begin to look "normal," leaving us feeling afraid, because our bodies don't measure up to what we see.

And for many, these altered images are viewed at a young age—a time when there is limited ability to think critically about what we see or to realize that very few, if any, women look like the images presented. As a result, unrealistic expectations for how one's body "should" look are formed and wired in the brain, at a time when young girls are experiencing tremendous pressure to measure up and fit in.

These unreasonable expectations, formed with an immature brain, often become the lens through which many women continue to evaluate how well their body measures up throughout their lives, leaving them in constant fear and in a struggle to make their body match these ideals—most often by trying to lose weight.

fear of being fat

As women, our biggest fear in not measuring up seems to be around weight. You may be the exception, and I haven't met a woman who doesn't fear getting fat or what it means about her that she is fat. In 2002, 33,000 American women told researchers that they would rather lose 10 to 15 pounds than achieve any other goal.[20]

That is an old statistic, and it is one worth taking a moment to think about. Making themselves smaller was more important than any other goal.

This is especially alarming in thinking about the stats that Jess Baker reports in 2015 regarding young girls. According to Baker, 91% of women are unhappy with their body and have resorted to dieting, and 81% of ten-year-old girls are afraid of getting fat—more afraid of getting fat than they are of cancer or losing their parents.[21]

Why is carrying extra weight so terrifying? With all that we hear about the dangers of obesity, one might assume that our fears stem from the health risks.

weight and health

The overweight women who have come to see me certainly have been concerned about the impact their extra weight was having on their health. Similar to Margaret, who I introduced you to at the beginning of the book, many women have worried about developing high blood pressure or diabetes.

With how often we hear that "obesity kills," you might believe, as most of my clients have, that the research solidly supports this claim. It doesn't.[22, 23, 24]

In some cases, carrying extra weight may in fact be protective. This is what has come to become known as the "obesity paradox." For instance, one study found that in-hospital mortality was highest in underweight patients while patients in the overweight category were less likely to die after the initial 30 days out and out to three years.[25] And factors such as fitness level and fruit and vegetable consumption may have more impact on health status and mortality than weight.[26]

Gaining this information has been a relief for women who have come to me fearing their weight was killing them. It has helped ease some of their stress.

And for these women, there was another layer. A layer of fear tied more to the approval of others than to their health-related concerns.

a sanctioned prejudice

As much as we worry about being politically correct, commenting disparagingly about a fat person's body seems to be "allowed" and maybe even encouraged. The justification is often something along the lines of, "Well, they should do something about it!"

What are your reactions to the word "fat?" Does it ignite fear, or maybe repulsion? If so, you are not alone. Women usually recoil when I use that term.

Why is that? Isn't fat simply a descriptor at the opposite end of the weight continuum from thin? Hardly. Fat has negative connotations of being lazy, unmotivated, uneducated, unclean, and/or lacking self-control. I'm sure I have missed a descriptor, and clearly, "fat" is not something women want to be.

This sanctioned prejudice—the daily comments or disparaging looks—takes a toll on self-worth, especially for a woman basing her worth on how others view her. Over time these critical comments become internalized with the result being both internal and external weight shaming.

We are learning that in addition to negatively impacting emotional health, weight stigmatization also seems to, *in and of itself,* be detrimental to physical health. The experience of being stigmatized or discriminated against because of size has been shown to negatively affect markers used to assess health such as lipid levels, glucose metabolism, and inflammation.[27]

Because these changes in health markers are most often attributed to the weight itself, women experience further incrimination and feel more internal shame, thereby further whittling away at their health and self-worth.

There is a movement for women to reclaim the word fat as simply a descriptor of size. And many women struggle with accepting the term preferring large or overweight because of the negative connotations of the word fat.

I think part of the problem is that people assume these terms are associated with being fat for good reason. This is what the women who have come to see me have believed—making comments about their weight such as:

"I lack motivation," or "I have no self-control," and "I guess I'm lazy or don't try hard enough."

These beliefs are certainly reinforced by what we see and hear through the media.

the diet industry

In 2019, weight loss industries spent 78 billion dollars[28], ensuring we know there is a way to lose weight and get the body we "should have." We are indoctrinated to believe that if we just work hard or follow the right plan, we can easily change the size and shape of our bodies. And if you change your body, you can be happy, beautiful, rich, and well, you name it.

We hear these messages so often that few people doubt them. It just seems true. If I tried harder, had more willpower, or more self-control, I would have the thin body I am supposed to have.

In reality, it is very difficult for almost everyone to lose weight and maintain that loss. The statistic most often quoted is that between 3-5 percent of those who lose weight will maintain that loss in the long term. Said another way, weight loss in the long-term has a 95 to 97 percent failure rate.

Yet the influence and power of these industries keep women believing that if you do it right, you can easily look as you "should" look. And if you don't, the problem is inside of you.

social forces and the fear of fat

Women didn't always fear being fat. At one time when food was less available, a large body was a sign of wealth and was envied. Women in paintings from the Renaissance would be considered fat by today's standards. Well-rounded bodies were preferred to lean or bony bodies.[29]

Social standards for beauty have certainly changed. One might assume that these changes have coincided with medical advances, longevity, and a resulting increased interest in health. Let's take a moment to consider perspectives more related specifically to the female experience.

Now that we, as women, have more freedoms and opportunities, is it possible we are now being held back from being ourselves and having more power by our pursuit of the perfect body? Have we traded one prison for another?

As Naomi Wolf, author of *The Beauty Myth* shares, women's obsession with physical perfection has now replaced the prison of only being allowed the option of being a wife and homemaker. She writes,

"The more legal and material hindrances women have broken through, the more strictly and heavily and cruelly images of female beauty have come to weigh on us."[30]

Many of my overweight female clients have shared experiences of being seen as "ineffectual" because of their size. Others have expressed fear around taking professional risks or "putting themselves out there" because of their weight.

In her book, *The Obsession*, Kim Chernin contends that women wishing to make their female parts smaller and less "apparent," may in fact be struggling with being female in this culture. She writes the following in the book description:

"This is a book about our veiled and often disguised obsession — with our right to be women in this culture, with our right to grow and develop ourselves, and to be accepted by our culture in a way that ceases to do damage to what we are, in our own most fundamental nature, as women."[31]

Twiggy, a model with a prepubescent body who came into fame in the sixties seems to exemplify this. Twiggy's nickname, prior to modeling, was "Twig" because she was as thin as a twig. Her designer dressed her to look like a pre-teen, and women's clothing started to be designed to look like children's clothes in adult sizes.

Women felt pressure to emulate Twiggy's body. Some even wrapped their breasts with Ace bandages to decrease the appearance of their size.[32]

This development coincided with the development of the birth control pill. For the first time, women experienced reproductive freedom. Women could now make a choice about pregnancy and enjoy sexual intimacy in a relaxed way, which had previously only been enjoyed by men.

And yet, women were being encouraged to dress like children. This might just be seen as a passing "fad." And what was the impact on women's psyche? How could a mature woman possibly feel good about her body when she was being sold the message that maturity wasn't attractive? Was this a move to stunt the fight toward autonomy?[33] And as Wolf asks, was Twiggy's thinness reassuring to men with "her suggestion of female weakness, asexuality, and hunger"?[34]

Whether the answer to those questions is yes or no, basing one's worth on the images sold to us as being ideal leaves many women feeling undeserving and hopeless. And could we be unwittingly buying into standards that maintain social hierarchies?

Sociologist Sabrina Strings, Ph.D., in her book, *Fearing the Black Body: The Racial Origins of Fat Phobia,*[35] conducted a detailed review of the fear of fat and found that despite what might be assumed, the origins of the anti-fat bias weren't born in the medical field.

Surprisingly they were instead born in racial science associating "fatness" with being "savage" and "Black."

From Strings:

"The image of fat black women as "savage" and "barbarous" has been used to both degrade black women and discipline white women."

If fat was associated with being Black and inferior, then White women were encouraged subtly and not so subtly to differentiate themselves through thinness.

This association between fatness and Blackness, along with its corresponding fear, was followed by Protestant moralism with its disdain of indulgence. The medical field only recently began contributing to our fear.

My point in talking about health and weight, as well as our fear of fat as it relates to race and being female, is to nudge you to look at why you want to be thin and your beliefs about what it means if you are not thin.

Thinness doesn't guarantee health. There are many unwell thin women. And there are many women who are making themselves unwell in their desperate attempt to meet societal standards for thinness.

Despite what the social forces of the day suggest, thinness doesn't equal anything but thinness. It doesn't guarantee anything except a lower number on the scale.

And, if you are going to separate your worth from approval, you are going to need to consider the standards that you are using to judge your body's "worth." If you believe you will only be worthwhile when you look a certain way or you are waiting to follow your dreams until you have the right body, you will likely miss out on a great deal in this one precious life of yours.

Especially because holding onto thin ideals engages so many women in a battle they never win.

a losing battle

Thin ideals wouldn't be so problematic if they were easy to achieve. I mentioned this before, and it is worth spending a bit more time looking at this in light of the number of women who believe they will be "good enough" if they can make their bodies smaller.

Marlene Schwartz, director of the Rudd Center for Food Policy and Obesity at the University of Connecticut (as cited by Sole-Smith), says:

> *"To give the impression that changing your weight status from obese to overweight or normal weight is this straightforward, easy thing to do is to effectively ignore 50 years of research."*[36]

Our bodies seem to have other ideas when it comes to decreasing our weight. The body is most concerned with surviving a famine and being prepared for the next one. It doesn't matter to the body whether the famine is self-imposed.

According to neuroscientist Sandra Aamodt, Ph.D., the physiology of our bodies defends against weight loss even if the starting weight would be considered obese. The brain's weight regulation system has two priorities: keeping body weight stable and not letting it decrease very much.[37]

She describes the human body as having a "one-way ratchet." This ratchet allows weight to go up and to not stay below what she describes as the body's "defended" range of weight.

This certainly seems to play out when one looks at the long-term ability to maintain weight loss. Traci Mann, Ph.D., and her team looked at studies of weight loss with follow-up periods between two to ten years and found that on average dieters had only lost two pounds and that nearly half (40 percent) *weighed more* than their starting weight at follow-up.[38]

Are these statistics hard to believe? Do you believe that if you could just find the right plan or have enough willpower, you could be thin? If so, you are certainly not alone.

Many capable, beautiful, and intelligent women spend their lives feeling unlovable or "not good enough" because they believe they should be able to attain societal expectations for thinness.

a terrible bind with terrible consequences

The pressure to be thin results in a terrible bind for most women. I wonder if you are feeling that bind after reading the last sections. Is there a part of you feeling angry at the pressures put on women regarding their bodies and maybe feeling validated in your failed attempts to change your body? And is there an even a larger part of you feeling terrified of separating your worth from the number on the scale? If so, that is understandable. The pressure to be thin is relentless and comes at us from every angle.

And I want to be clear that I am not saying that you shouldn't lose weight if that is what you want for yourself or you have been advised to do so by your physician. Your body is your body, and it is your choice.

What is problematic is the connection between your worth and a number on the scale or a certain size of pants. You may be in the minority and have a body that meets our thin ideals, and what happens when you are pregnant or when other hormonal changes like those that come with aging redefine your size or shape?

When worth is measured by size, your worth will feel precarious. Changes in weight, failing to lose weight, or the inability to maintain weight loss are likely going to leave you feeling anxious, depressed, and unworthy.

Being dissatisfied with one's weight can also lead to weight cycling or "yo-yo" dieting, a tendency to diet, regain, and then diet again. As you can imagine, this pattern certainly takes a toll emotionally. It also appears to have health consequences as well.[39]

Feeling stressed about the size of your body can become self-defeating when it comes to weight. The more stressed we are about our weight, the more likely we will struggle with it. Here's what I mean by that. If I am stressed by the size of my body, the stress hormones will trigger the body to hold on to fat stores. It is one of the ways the body protects itself.

And so, if you are stressing about the size of your body, you are likely, ensuring that your body will hold onto its fat stores and even attempt to increase those stores to be prepared for danger, including famine.

And what else happens when you are stressed? Do you find yourself eating when it is the very thing you don't want to do?

We will talk much more about this throughout the book, and when you are stressed the parts of the brain running the show pull us toward immediate relief with no awareness of the consequences of our actions. Stressing about the size of your body often leads to the very overeating that you are trying to avoid. Being dissatisfied with your body has other consequences as well.

Being dissatisfied with one's weight has been linked with poorer health behaviors and health status[40] and may also be associated with obesity-related comorbidities such as the risk of developing Type II diabetes, regardless of BMI.[41] In other words, *being dissatisfied with weight was a stronger predictor of developing Type II diabetes than was weight.*

Compounding these emotional and physical difficulties is the fear of being judged by a health care provider. If you are overweight, do you avoid seeking help, including medical help, because of the shame you feel about your weight and your fear of being judged because of it? This was the experience of most of my female overweight clients.

There was also the fear of being told to lose weight because many knew they had been unable to do so in the past and worried about yet another failure and the accompanying embarrassment of not having been "compliant."

For a woman who finds her worth in approval, this is a terrible bind. I want to keep you, as my provider, happy. I will feel good about myself if you are happy with me, and no matter how hard I try I can't get to the thin person you want me to be.

the powerful need to please and appease

I hope that what I have shared with you so far in this chapter has triggered you to think about why we, as women, may have such strong conscious and unconscious needs to seek approval.

I also hope it has widened and shifted your perspective, moving you from a place of feeling personally defective to an awareness and appreciation of the strong forces at play, driving women to look outside themselves for value.

I didn't share this information to leave you feeling a victim or trapped by societal pressures. These pressures are real. I share this information to normalize connections you may have between your self-worth and the approval of others.

Based on our history and experience as women, of course we have these connections. And if you believe that your worth is measured by how thin you are, of course you would want to be thin. How could you not struggle with body image in our culture?

We are constantly bombarded with how we should look, and yet very few women meet these ideals presented to us as "normal."

If you are overweight, of course you would believe that you are not good enough—our culture enforces that assumption. I'm quite sure you live with constant subtle and not so subtle criticisms, prejudice, and comments about your weight. There are most likely constant reminders that your body is not as it "should" be whether it comes to finding clothes that fit or a chair that will be comfortable to sit in.

And we as women are a part of this culture. We are a huge source of income for the big industries that rely on us believing that we are not okay as we are. Unfortunately, most women believe they are the problem—believing they are too weak or lacking the motivation to achieve these standards, and so they continue to strive to conform rather than confront these unreasonable standards expected of them.

As I will talk about in the next section, these pressures to please or be chosen also pit one woman against the next, robbing us of true support from other women for being ourselves—thus preventing us from standing together as a united force against these societal pressures.

We cannot change other people, and we can change what we believe. What might happen if each of us, as women, worked on our own beliefs about our bodies? What if our bodies became our home, our source of life and opportunity rather than a measuring stick of our worth?

In writing this, I am reminded of a powerful moment in my doctoral training at the University of Northern Colorado, when my professor, David M. Gonzalez, Ph.D., responded to a student feeling overwhelmed and powerless after listening to the experiences of the disenfranchised. It has been many years now since hearing Dr. Gonzalez's response, and so it is quite likely these words are more my memory than his actual words.

David suggested that each of us be a candle of light by doing what we can in our own lives to treat all human beings with respect. By being that light, we would likely light the candles of those around us. Together, in that classroom, we imagined how much light there would be if each of us was a candle of light.

I wonder what might be possible if we, as women, took it upon ourselves to shine a light of acceptance on our bodies and the bodies of those around us. I know I would like to live in the glow of that light. How about you?

And if that sounds good and you have no idea how you would get to a place of self-acceptance, hold on. I will help you with that in part two of the book.

the power of perception

While certainly not denying that these societal pressures and prejudices exist, what's also true is that our perceptions are determined by our beliefs. If I believe that I need to avoid disapproval, my brain will be actively looking for signs of disapproval.

As you will discover in chapter nineteen, many of my client's expectations for how others would react turned out to be false. They had been interpreting the behavior of others in a way that matched their assumptions.

We see what we expect to see, and the brain makes this easier for us by applying old assumptions to the current situation—trying to predict what will be helpful in the present moment based on what was "true" in the past. We will talk much more about this in part two.

The truth of life is that you will likely be judged for being yourself in the world. We all judge. We decide if we like or don't like something. As much as I would like to say that I like all people equally, that isn't true. There are some people I am drawn to, and others that I'm not.

These choices are about my likes and dislikes and what feels comfortable to me. They say nothing about the worth of those who fall outside of my preferences. If it is hard for you to believe that someone's disapproval is about them and not you, that is understandable. Most of the women working on this pattern struggled with this idea in the beginning.

It is also important to recognize that these patterns or expectations about what it means to be loved or accepted don't define you—they simply reflect well-traveled circuits or "wiring" in the brain. It is important to separate who we are from what we have wired in our brains.

Most women realize they have very different expectations for their friends or daughters than they have for themselves. I think of these beliefs as separate highways in the brain. You might be on one highway believing you need the approval of others to be okay, or on another, encouraging your daughter to be herself. These are simply different pathways in the brain.

Neither of these define you. They simply reflect what is lighting up in the brain. Our nervous system and our level of stress has a great deal to do with how we react and experience events in our lives. We will come back to this, and for those of you wondering how you can encourage your daughter to be herself and at the same time struggle with accepting yourself, I hope this sheds some light.

And it is important to realize that there is hope because the brain is constantly changing. In the next section we will talk more about the brain and the possibilities for change, and first let's stop and take a moment to review and give you a chance to reflect.

in a nutshell

- Because we are constantly bombarded with images of women that have been altered to perfection, this type of perfection starts to define what is normal and leaves women in fear of never measuring up.

- To make matters worse, most of us draw conclusions about how we should look when we are young and before our brains have fully developed—before we have the ability to think critically about what we are seeing.

- As a result, we develop unreasonable assumptions about appearance and how we should look. These assumptions become wired in the brain and act as the template for assessing whether our bodies are "good enough."

- Women's biggest fear in measuring up seems to be around weight. This fear traps women in a lifelong losing battle with their worth hanging precariously on a clothes size or number on a scale.

- Now that we, as women, have more freedoms and opportunities, are we allowing ourselves to be held back from expansion, influence, and power by spending our time in the pursuit of the perfect body?

- I hope what I have shared with you in this chapter has widened and shifted your perspective, moving you from a place of feeling personally defective to an awareness and an appreciation of the strong forces at play, driving the connection between worth and approval.

- I didn't share this information to leave you feeling a victim or trapped by societal pressures. The pressures are real. And we as women are a part of this culture and a large source of income for the industries enforcing these standards.

- What might happen if each of us as women worked on our own beliefs about our bodies—if our bodies became our home, our source of life and opportunity rather than a measuring stick of our worth?

- How might our lives and the world change if each of us became a light of acceptance for our own body and the bodies of those around us?

- It is also true that our beliefs determine what we will see. If I believe I am undeserving, I will see myself in that way.

- Old assumptions typically get in the way of changing how we see ourselves. The brain applies old assumptions to current situations—trying to predict what will be helpful in the present moment based on what was "true" in the past.

- The good news is that you are not what you have wired in your brain. These assumptions about your worth are simply well-traveled circuits or "wiring" in the brain, and the brain is constantly changing based on what we do, think, and feel.

We will talk more about that in the next section.

ideas for reflection

- When and how did you learn what it means to be attractive?

- What pressures have you felt around your appearance or your weight?

- In what ways do you seek approval through your appearance?

- What associations do you have with the word "fat?"

- What reactions did you have to the ideas presented about weight and social hierarchies?

- If you have tried unsuccessfully to lose weight, what assumptions have you made about yourself?

- Take some time to think about your relationships. What qualities do you look for in a friend? Do any of these qualities have to do with appearance?

- How do the standards you hold for yourself around weight or appearance differ from those you hold for your daughter or a good friend? What was it like to realize that these standards simply reflect different pathways in the brain?

- How might you use the information presented in this chapter to reconsider some of your assumptions about weight and appearance? What is an action you might take?

- How might you light a candle of body acceptance in your own life?

chapter two
part three

the brain is constantly changing

We now know that the brain is constantly changing based on what we think, feel, and do. It was once believed that by the time we reach adulthood our brain was fixed or unchangeable.

We now know that it is possible to change the structure of our brain. This is called neuroplasticity. When we purposely change our behaviors or reactions with enough regularity to change the pathways in our brain, this is called self-directed neuroplasticity.

We likely have barely scratched the surface of possibility when it comes to using our mind to change our brain or our body. As new advances in technology allow us to view what is happening in the brain in real time, we are learning how our behaviors, thoughts, feelings, and even our imagination can change the brain.

In my "welcome" I shared with you one of the studies Sharon Begley includes in her book *Train your Mind Change Your Brain*, illustrating how imagination alone led to changes in the structure of the brain. I want to share another study that is more directly related to changing thoughts and reactions. In this study, neuro-psychiatrist Jeffery Schwartz demonstrated that how we think and what we pay attention to changes what happens in the brain, as well as the symptoms of obsessive-compulsive disorder (OCD).

He used a PET scan to look at the brains of patients who previously had moderate to severe OCD and who had experienced significant relief after mindfulness-based therapy.

He found that the therapy had changed the faulty OCD circuit in the brain and concluded that "willful, mindful effort can alter brain function and that self-directed brain changes—self-directed neuroplasticity—are a genuine reality." He went on to say, *the mind can change the brain.*"[42]

We will talk much more about this in part two, and I hope you find this both exciting and hopeful. Once you can notice when your wires linking approval with your worth are lighting up, you have the chance to bring new information into them. Doing this with enough repetition gives you the chance to change your beliefs connecting your worth with the approval of others.

you don't need to stop caring

I wonder as you are reading this if fear is coming up around what it will mean to change these wires?

Clients often wonder if working on this pattern means they will need to stop being a caring person. The answer is, absolutely not. Your caring and sensitivity are gifts to the world. Women's ability to keep the peace and "play nice" are some of the wonderful contributions the feminine brings to the world and some of the reasons we need more female voices.

We are working on separating your worth from the approval of others. This wiring leads you to believe that *to be valuable and have worth, you must please others.* If you don't, you will be alone.

So, when I talk about this pattern or intimacy style, I am not talking about *choosing* to be kind, thoughtful, or nice. I am talking about keeping people happy because *your self-worth depends on it* — which can feel like your life depends on it.

Keeping others happy to feel safe and "okay," is very different from choosing to be kind and generous.

Yes, I want you to be the caring, loving person you are! And it can't stay wired with your self-worth or with safety. You will never climb out of stress or feel like you are "enough."

No matter how hard you try, you are never going to "keep people happy." Because you can't make people happy in the first place.

you can't make people happy

What is your reaction to that statement? Do you disagree? If so, you are certainly not alone. Even our use of language supports the idea that we can make people feel a certain way. It is common to hear statements like, "She made me mad." Or "He made me sad." I was working with a client feeling exhausted from trying to keep the people in her life happy. She didn't buy the idea that she couldn't "make people happy." She truly believed that as a wife, it was her job to *"keep her husband happy"* and that she could do this if she tried.

I asked,

"What about those times when you work hard fixing him his favorite supper, one you just know he will enjoy, and he walks in the door mad as a hornet about something from work? Is your dinner going to make him happy?"

A lightbulb went on. She said,

"Oh, now I get it. I can do things I think will make him happy, but that doesn't mean he will be happy."

Her internal wiring had been telling her the opposite: that she "could and should make him happy" and as a result, she was feeling stressed, overwhelmed, and anxious.

She could never get to the place where she could relax. There was always the chance she would disappoint someone. Even when she had time to herself, she couldn't relax. Her sense of being "okay" was totally entangled with getting approval from others.

when is it enough?

When you depend on things outside of yourself to feel good, competent, successful, or safe, when do you arrive? When is it good enough?

How can you really relax? Even if people are happy with you today, will they feel the same way tomorrow?

Or, as Margaret said,

"I never feel like I get to the place where I have done enough and can relax."

There are always the what ifs:
- What if I missed something important?
- What if my partner leaves me?
- What if I disappoint my boss and lose my job?
- What if I regain the weight I lost?

There is a vulnerability that is always there. Or, as one client described it,

"It feels fragile. I never quite trust that it will continue."

Can you see how this vulnerability or fragility would trigger fear and a pull to keep working harder?

Fear triggers a sense of danger in the brain. In danger, it's impossible to relax even if you want to.

safety is necessary for relaxation and growth

Feeling safe is necessary for relaxation and for growth. It is essential. It is a matter of physiology. Think about it. If you are being chased by a lion, are you going to be sitting down to relax or thinking about career choices or how to give your life meaning?

I imagine you might be chuckling thinking about this because it is so obvious.

The same thing is true no matter what the stressor is in your life, whether it's a lion or continually trying to stay on top of things so that people will see you in a positive light. If this wiring is insisting that you please the people in your life, stress will be a constant in your life.

We cannot grow, think creatively, or even plan effectively in the middle of the stress response.

why this is especially important today

Working on this entangled style of relating is critical in today's world. We are constantly bombarded with images and messages of how we should be. It is extremely difficult to avoid this constant input. If this old wiring stays in place you are going to find yourself continually triggered and afraid.

And women today face questions that the women who came before us never imagined.

Questions like:

- What career path will I choose?
- If I have a career, will I be a good mother?
- Is it enough for me to stay home and focus on being a mother?
- If I choose not to have children, what does that say about me and about being a woman?

Food still has to be on the table, bills paid, kids taken care of, with all the activities that come along with that. And now we face larger questions that were never on the radar, questions like:

- What will be my life's purpose?
- How will I create a life with meaning?
- How will I leave the world a better place?

All of which sit squarely on top of the responsibilities that have always been there. Can you feel that? It's a lot, right?

If you add this intimacy style—this unconscious need to keep everyone happy and approving of you—wired at the level of your life depending on it, how in the world can you not be overwhelmed, stressed, and anxious?

I don't think it is possible. It is a dead-end street. One that only leads to feeling overwhelmed, stressed, depressed, and hopeless.

We have to look at this invisible force driving us to attempt the impossible and leaving us feeling as if we constantly have a hill to climb while lacking sure footing.

my wish

I want something different for all women feeling trapped by the need for approval and the pressure it brings with it to be and do more.

My hope is for you to feel relaxed and safe enough, just as you are, to bloom into the radiant being you were meant to be in this world! And doing that is going to mean working on this old wiring keeping you anxious and overwhelmed.

changing the collective female consciousness

As we learn more about how our individual energy impacts those around us, what a difference we might make in the experience of being female if we were to each work on this invisible pull to seek approval. The force to gain approval and to be chosen, by its very nature, pits women against each other. It leads us to compare ourselves to one another, hoping that we measure up or exceed what we see.

We want to be chosen.

Have you found yourself checking out how other women look as you enter a room and making comparisons with how you look? If so, you are certainly not alone. I hear this over and over from the women who come to see me.

My clients who have shared making these types of comparisons felt guilty and ashamed for having done so. Yet they found themselves continuing to compare, hoping to come out on top.

We seem to feel better about ourselves when we believe we look better, or at least not worse, than other women. This is understandable in light of our early socialization to attract and be chosen. And, if we believe other women are thinner, or otherwise more attractive, it can zap our confidence and spoil our mood. As a client shared with me,

"My internal diatribes about a tiny butt woman on the ski hill ruined my whole day on the mountain, and I'm still angry thinking about her."

In this way, it pits us against each other. Has this happened in your life? Have you felt angry toward a woman who seemingly had what you believed you should have?

Does your fear of being inferior lead to an internal dialogue that makes it difficult for you to enjoy being with or to celebrate the women around you?

For my client, that "tiny-butt woman" became the enemy; she had what my client believed would make her "good and acceptable." She felt embarrassed by her thoughts, and in rational moments, recognized that this woman most likely had her own struggles. And it felt so very unfair. It was hard for her to let go of her anger.

Finding our self-worth in approval robs us of the support of other women. When we are in constant competition, how can there be true support?

And quantum physics tells us that we are not the solid beings we imagine ourselves to be. Instead, we are vibrating energy. Our thoughts and emotions are also in the form of energy and become a part of the energetic database of the human consciousness.[43]

Looked at in this way, the energy of the thoughts and feelings of each woman add to the database of the female consciousness. My vision is a shift in the energy of that collective female consciousness from one of fear and competition to one of true support.

I imagine this happening as each of us works on separating our worth from the approval of others. What might be possible if the female experience could shift from a fear-based energy, driving us to compete, to one that is firmly rooted in the safety of our own wisdom and supported by a powerful connection with other women as allies rather than competitors?

I recognize that this shift in the female consciousness doesn't change social pressures, violence against women, or misogyny. And could we make a larger difference if we were united? If we felt supported by other women in being ourselves and if we supported other women in being themselves, as well?

And if we weren't constantly scrambling, fearfully, for approval, would we be more open, more receptive to larger sources of support in the universe that have always been there?

I imagine so many possibilities could open up if we stepped out of the stress coming from this pull to define our worth by other's approval.

And, even if it simply decreased your stress or gave you some peace, wouldn't it be worth it?

in a nutshell

- We now know that it is possible to change the structure of our brains by changing how we think, feel, and behave. It is even possible to make changes using your imagination.

- Noticing when your wires linking approval with your worth are lighting up, and bringing new information into them with enough repetition gives you the opportunity to change the beliefs connecting your worth with the approval of others.

- In doing this work, you are not working on changing how much you care. Keeping others happy to feel safe and "okay," is very different from choosing to be kind and generous.

- Despite the pull to "make it happen," keeping people happy is an impossible job. You can't make people happy.

- Striving to keep others happy leaves you vulnerable and stressed. If you have approval today, will you have it tomorrow?

- If this wiring is insisting that you please the people in your life, stress will be a constant, and it will be impossible to relax, be creative, or ask larger questions such as, "What is the life I want for myself?"

- Because of this, if you want to feel more secure and able to relax, working on this style of relating is going to be essential.

- This striving for approval pits women against each other. Working on separating your worth from how others see you may allow you to feel truly supported by other women and open you up to sources of support in the universe that were always there and have gone unnoticed as you worked so hard to gain approval.

ideas for reflection

- How was it to learn that these pulls to look outside yourself for your value simply reflect well-traveled circuits in the brain and that the structure of your brain is changeable?

- What came up for you when I said you can't make other people happy or control their feelings?

- In what ways do you find yourself comparing yourself with other women?

- Take a moment to imagine a life in which you could be yourself and feel supported by the women in your life. What would it feel like and look like? How would you be acting, behaving, and relating?

If that is hard for you to imagine, no worries, we will work on that in part two.

chapter three
much study; many women; many years

Once while talking with a client about these patterns of relating, she asked me,

"So, did you come up with the idea of the entangled intimacy style all on your own?"

Since she asked me, I'm imagining some of you may be wondering the same thing. So, before we move on, I'd like to answer that question for you, as well.

I really have my clients to thank for helping me recognize this pattern. Without their willingness to share their struggles, I wouldn't have noticed this recurring pattern.

And my education and training also played a big part.

the shoulders I stand on

I first became interested in styles of relating while working on my doctorate. I was taking a family systems class, and we were studying Murray Bowen, M.D. I felt fascinated by a sentence in my textbook describing Bowen's theories. I no longer have that textbook, and what I remember was this thought.

When young adults move across the country to be independent, they may in fact be less independent (differentiated) than those who can live near their parents and totally be themselves. Even if being themselves leads to disapproval or conflict.

The idea was surprising and confusing. I didn't know how anyone could do that. It was a question that stayed with me because it didn't fit with my experience.

Bowen's scale of differentiation

In differentiation of self, Bowen was describing a process of individual development that happens within relationships or the family unit. High differentiation is the ability to be oneself while maintaining emotional contact.[44]

Or in other words to stay true to oneself while maintaining emotional connection. Bowen's ideas were foundational in my thinking about the patterns I was noticing in my clients.

Laurel Mellin's merging and distancing

Laurel Mellin, Ph.D.,[45] reconnected me with my memories of Bowen in her descriptions of merging and distancing.

Dr. Mellin was ahead of her time in her work on emotional regulation, using principles of neuroscience. I trained with her and ran groups teaching clients her brain-based regulation skills.

Dr. Mellin's work focuses on identifying and shifting brain states in order to wire the brain for joy versus stress. Merging and distancing were associated with states of stress.

a collective experience

In sitting with women over the years, I began to think of the concepts of differentiation, merging and distancing on a larger scale—in the experience of being female.

While theorists such as Bowen have described certain types of families that inhibit differentiation, maybe in a similar way society, our history and socialization as women, and even the collective female consciousness have inhibited women's differentiation through a terrible fear of being abandoned if we were to displease. This fear may be learned and passed down through what I have come to call an entangled intimacy style.

you say potāto; I say potâto

You may read about the entangled intimacy style and think it sounds like something someone else described in another way. Or some of you may think, "This is just another way of talking about codependency."

One thing I have learned from all the years working as a licensed psychologist is that there are many ways of describing the same thing. Various theoretical perspectives use different words to describe the same life processes or experiences.

To different people, some ways of describing things just makes more sense than other ways of describing things.

Describing this pattern in the terms of an entangled intimacy style has been helpful for the women who have come to see me. Since it has been helpful to them, I am hoping it will be helpful to you, as well.

my personal experience

As I share personal experiences, please know I share them feeling no judgment of my parents and family. I love them dearly and feel blessed for all they gave me. As is true of all parents, my parents were people with their own gifts and challenges. I know they loved me and wanted the best for me.

And I was an active participant in my learning. I made sense of what I heard with my immature brain. When we are young, our brain is still developing. It is not until our mid-twenties that the most advanced part of the brain, the neocortex is fully developed. This more advanced part of the brain, which I will call the thinking brain, allows us to think critically and evaluate what we see and hear.

Prior to that, the more primitive parts of the brain, which I will call the emotional brain, are running the show. As children, we are trying to make sense of an enormous amount of information with a brain that lacks the ability to put things in perspective.

As a result, in childhood, our thinking is very concrete. We make sense of things as either good or bad—right or wrong. It is difficult for a child to see the "gray" without the help of an adult. If I can't throw the ball, I will *never* be able to throw the ball.

And we are very egocentric. For instance, children often feel responsible for divorce, feeling that somehow it was their fault. And if a parent is disappointed or angry, a child will often decide this means something about them. "I must be bad for him to be angry."

The beliefs that we develop during this stage of our development often take the form of "if this then that." Part of this has to do with what we hear as children—statements like, "If you don't do your homework then you can't go out to play." Or "If you don't eat your vegetables then you can't have dessert."

Other times we draw conclusions of our own. For instance, a mother might say, without giving it much thought, "It would make me so happy if you cleaned your room and her child might decide, "If I do what people want, then they will be happy with me."

And we often draw sweeping generalizations from a single incident that had nothing to do with us. For instance, a child might decide, "Nothing I do makes a difference" when her father comes home from work after learning his company is downsizing and ignores her when she finally got the good grade he had been nudging her to work for.

In neither case did the parent intend for their child to make these assumptions and most likely they were unaware that their child was making them.

Now to be clear, I'm not meaning to negate your experience if your parent(s) were cruel or abusive in their treatment of you. Sometimes, the words are said directly, and we take them in, and they become the template or the lens through which we see the world.

Either way it is the outdated unreasonable learning or the lens that needs to be updated or made more reasonable.

And, if you are a parent and you are worried about things you may have said to your children, I want to remind you that you don't have to be perfect to be a good parent and that we all end up in adulthood with crossed wires we need to work on.

I would encourage you to focus on yourself. As you learn to take better care of yourself, you will model this behavior for your children.

Okay, back to my experience.

an introvert in a family of extroverts with an entangled intimacy style

I grew up as an introvert in a family of extroverts. Well, except for my father who, sadly, didn't realize that he was fine just as he was, reading a book or out puttering in his shop.

When I use the term introvert, I am referring to how I "charge my batteries" and not to the common misperception of introversion relating to "shyness." Introverts charge their batteries through spending time alone, whereas extroverts do so by being with other people. During my teenage years, when I was busy working on solitary projects, my pull to those activities was often questioned. What I heard was that I was doing something wrong and that what I enjoyed wasn't "normal."

I understand, now, that from an extrovert's perspective my solitary and creative activities seemed strange, and it was hard from an extrovert's perspective to see my pull toward those interests as "normal."

What I didn't realize was the powerful force at play—the force of an entangled intimacy style. All I knew was that I felt a horrible internal struggle. If I loved them, then I couldn't be myself. This wasn't a conscious struggle. I felt it.

As I shared with you, connection is a survival need. So, my brain chose connection over being myself. Because I spent so much of my early years trying to keep other people happy, I didn't know who I was or what was important to me.

I feel sad thinking of all the time I lost not knowing who I was in the world. The good news is that it wasn't too late. It was too late for some things and not too late to make a difference in my life.

Changing this entangled style of relating is a journey I have traveled and continue to travel. As I work on changing this pattern, sometimes I am better at doing things differently than I am at other times. I imagine the same will be true for you.

And I can be gentle with myself in a way that wasn't possible before. Even on the days when I fall back into measuring how I am doing based on how others react, I can be kind to myself. This alone moves me out of stress and into a more balanced state.

you are wonderful as you are

There is nothing "wrong" with you if you have learned this intimacy style. If you see yourself in the examples I share, I hope you know that you are not alone. Many women share this pattern, and you are not defective for having learned this way of relating.

The beliefs driving these patterns were most likely developed when you were young and doing your best to make sense of the world with an immature brain. These patterns of relating have likely become default wiring in your brain and if so, remember that your wiring doesn't define you. Judging by my experience with the women who came to see me with this pattern, I'm betting you are a caring, capable, intuitive woman.

So, try not to be hard on yourself. See if you can be curious about whether what I share describes you. And if it does, that's fantastic! You will now understand why "getting there" always seems "out of reach."

In the next chapter, let's start looking more closely at the components of this style of relating.

in a nutshell

- The idea of an entangled intimacy style grew from the experiences my clients shared with me and from my education and training.

- Beliefs about ourselves and about relationships are primarily formed during childhood. During this time, we take in enormous amounts of information and try to make sense of it with an immature brain.

- As a result, the conclusions we make are concrete or they are either/or, such as good or bad. They lack a "wide-lens" perspective. For instance, "If you are unhappy with me, I'm not lovable or okay."

- Beliefs also often take the form of "if this, then that." For instance, "If I am good, then you will be happy and love me."

- And sometimes children hear directly from adults that they are not good enough, or are worthless, and this becomes the lens through which they see the world.

- Either way, it is the outdated or unreasonable learning or the lens that needs work.

- Growing up with an entangled intimacy style can get in the way of you learning who you are and what is important to you.

- And it is possible to notice this pattern and to begin discovering who you are and were meant to be in this world.

ideas for reflection

- What messages did you receive about being yourself when you were young?
- Did you have a sense there was a way you "should be?" In what ways did you get this message?
- What impact have those messages had on you and your life?

chapter four

appeasing: the heart and soul of the entangled intimacy style

Okay, let's start looking more closely at the entangled intimacy style. Appeasing is at the core of this intimacy style. Merriam-Webster defines appeasing as: "to bring a state of peace, quiet or calm; to pacify; to make concessions often at the sacrifice of principles."[46]

I chose the word "appease" versus "please" because in this intimacy style women often sacrifice their own needs for the approval of others. Defining self-worth and love by how well you keep others happy is at the core of this intimacy style.

As a result of the pull to appease, women with this style of relating often "merge" with others. In an entangled style of relating, my identity can become merged with yours and I lose myself in you. As you will see in my client examples, women with this style of relating often lose their identity in relationships because their focus is on the needs of others.

Even though there is a powerful drive to seek approval in this style of relating, most women can only keep pleasing others for so long. Because of this, most swing between appeasing and disconnecting. I like to think of this as a pendulum swinging between appeasing on one side and disconnecting on the other.

the swinging pendulum

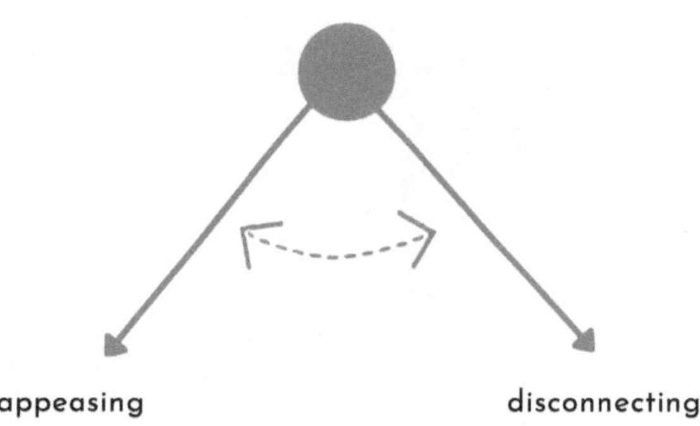

Women with an entangled intimacy style often swing from appeasing to disconnecting and back to appeasing.

If you don't find yourself relating to appeasing, it may be that you tend to spend more time disconnecting. We will talk about disconnecting in the next chapter. For now, let's start with appeasing.

appeasing

Appeasing is what most of us with this style of intimacy have learned about what it means to care and connect with other people.

It is also how you know you are doing a "good job," and how you know you are a "good, lovable person."

In appeasing, my focus is on you and your needs. If you have this intimacy style, you probably don't even realize this is your focus. It just feels "right," kind, or polite.

The pull to appease can also show up regarding women's appearance, career choice, or other decisions like whether to have children. Let's start with how it shows up in relationships.

To do that I will share an example of appeasing in my life when I was much younger and a graduate student at Penn State. At the time, I was feeling overwhelmed by the pressures of graduate school and one of my advisors suggested that grad students often benefited from the support offered at the counseling center.

I decided to check it out. It was my first experience in therapy. During one of our sessions, near the end of my time there and while I was sharing something that upset me, my therapist got up and started watering and trimming his plants.

I didn't know what to do, and so I just kept on talking while he seemingly ignored me and took care of his plants. I must have eventually said something, as I remember him saying,

"Oh, thank you! I thought I was going to have to stand here all session doing this to get you to speak up."

In my defense, I'd like to say the reason I didn't speak up was that it was my first experience in therapy. I had no frame of reference.

Maybe this was normal. And this wasn't a novice therapist, he was a member of the senior staff which made him a bit intimidating.

In reality, at that point in my life, I would have responded the same way if it was a beginning therapist on their first day at the job! My reasons may have differed, and my response would have been the same.

How about you? How would you respond? Some of you may have gotten angry. If so, we'll talk about that in the next chapter. Let's look more closely at what was happening within me. I remember feeling confused and wondering what he was doing.

My thoughts went something like this:

"Maybe he thinks better on his feet. Maybe he has been sitting all day and really needs to stand up."

Or something along those lines. Do you notice where I was focusing my attention and thoughts? I was focusing on what he might have been feeling and needing.

I am sure that I had thoughts about myself like:

"What am I supposed to do here? How am I supposed to handle this?"

I wanted to be a "good" client. This is one example of appeasing.

isn't that about assertiveness?

You might wonder, "Isn't that not being assertive?" And the answer is yes. And I have to know what I need and want in order to be assertive.

If I have an entangled intimacy style, when I am being pulled by the force to appease, my focus will be on the other person's needs, in this case my therapist, and being a good client. I will be disconnected from my own needs and so have little or no awareness of them.

This is not a thought-out process. It is not coming from the part of the brain responsible for conscious decisions. It has been practiced so often that it is automatic and happens without our awareness.

Let me digress for a moment and talk about default wiring.

how the brain helps us get through our days

Although we think we are consciously deciding moment by moment what we will do next, this isn't true. Most of what we do during our day is happening outside of our conscious awareness and results from default or procedural wiring in the brain.

This allows us to accomplish all that we do during a day. If we had to think about and direct everything that we did, we would all still be in bed.

Think about it. How would you direct your body to get out of bed? Where would you start? Would you start by telling your eyelids to open? Can you imagine how many steps it would take if you had to direct that action? Or think about heading out to your car. Do you think of the steps necessary to get in your car and get it moving? Maybe if you are a new driver.

I remember sitting with my nephew when he was learning to drive and watching him go through the steps to be ready to drive. He consciously fastened his seat belt; he checked all the mirrors; he looked for the spot for the key and put it in. Can you picture it? He thought before taking each step.

What if your day was like that for every single thing you did? We wouldn't get much done, would we? So, the brain makes it easy for us. Things we do repeatedly get "wired" in our brains, making it possible for us to do them without conscious thought. Most of us can get out of bed without thinking about it and eat breakfast while reading or talking to others. And unfortunately, most of us can drive without thinking about it.

This kind of default wiring happens in all areas of our lives. We learn some of it through experience, and some is passed down to us from our ancestors. Understanding how patterns of thought and behavior can become default networks in our brain helps to explain why I didn't speak up with my first therapist.

why didn't I speak up?

As I am writing this I'm thinking,

"What in the world? Why didn't I say something right away?"

I couldn't. It wasn't even in my awareness to do it differently. And if you have this style of relating, it most likely isn't in yours, either. Patterns of relating to others, just like other patterns such as the steps to driving a car, get wired in the brain and become automatic and operate outside of our conscious awareness. Growing up, when my brain chose keeping others happy over being an individual, that pattern formed and became a default.

By the time I sat there with that therapist, my unconscious patterns of relating were automatic, just like driving a car. Make sense? And because connection is associated with survival, the thought of changing it can bring up fear.

connection is a survival need

Have you noticed any fear coming up as you think about separating your self-worth from approval? If so, you aren't alone.

Remember Margaret who was struggling with staying on top of things? She compared herself to others and felt everyone was more organized than she could ever be.

When Margaret gained awareness of her tendency to appease, she felt afraid thinking about working on this tendency. At the heart of her fear was the following core belief:

"To be 'okay' and a good person, I need to keep people happy. If I don't, I won't be loved, and I will be alone."

Now, I'm not talking about rational thought. Margaret understood this wasn't workable. And, when she thought about changing it, she felt intense fear. Her brain had wired together keeping people happy with safety and survival.

I share this with you because if you have this intimacy style, you may very well feel this same fear. You may know the belief makes no sense and still feel fear when you think about changing it. You may also feel frustrated to realize that you feel afraid to change something that clearly isn't working in your life. Understanding the importance the brain places on anything related to survival may help you let go of the frustration, guilt, or shame you may be feeling.

The brain doesn't take survival lightly. We wouldn't have survived as a species if our ancestor's brains hadn't made powerful connections between things that kept them safe and things that were dangerous. Remember that early in our history as humans, to be cast out of the tribe was to die. Although we can live independently today, we carry with us those fears of our ancestors leaving most of us fearful of rejection.

And as children we are totally dependent on our caregivers. Because of this, anything that we decide will keep us loved and cared for will be wired with a connection to survival and safety. These wires related to safety are wired in a sturdy way.

To understand what I mean by this, think about the urge to run from a burning building. It would be automatic, right? Not a lot of thinking involved. And we probably couldn't talk ourselves out of doing it, right? The connection between fire and danger has been sturdily wired in our brains.

If you have this intimacy style, this learning is going to be wired in a similar sturdy way.

We will come back to this, and for now I hope it helps to normalize any fear that might be coming up as you think about changing these patterns.

And I will help you learn how to deal with this fear so that you feel safe to change these patterns in part two. For now, let's go back to me with my first therapist.

I was appeasing without realizing it, and I had no awareness of what he was trying to point out to me. I was busy trying to figure out:

- why he was doing what he was doing and
- what I was supposed to do about it, so I would be a "good" client

This was my entangled intimacy style at work. I needed to assess the situation and figure out how to be a good client.

it's not about being nice

If this is your intimacy style, I imagine that you are a kind and loving person who is more than willing to help other people. This is one of the gifts of this intimacy style.

I chose this example because I was seeing the therapist for a service. Granted, counseling was free for students, and he was there to help me. And my needs were nowhere in the picture.

I wasn't thinking, *"This is frustrating!"* or *"Why isn't he listening to me?"*

It has been a long time since I sat in that room, and I can tell you, my frustration had to do with figuring out *what was I supposed to be doing*, rather than that he was ignoring me.

This is a cornerstone of this style of intimacy. Your focus is on the other person and what they need and how to be a "good" client, wife, employee, girlfriend, or friend.

Let me give you another example by sharing a bit about my client Karen.

Karen and identity

Karen saw my flyer about healing your relationship with food and your body. Karen was in her late 30's, and happily married with two children. She was successful in her career. Losing weight had been her nemesis. She gained weight after getting married, and nothing had made a difference. She had had enough of dieting and was ready to try a fresh approach.

In the beginning of our work together, Karen struggled with identifying her feelings or stating what she needed from the people in her life. Through her work in therapy Karen became more adept at identifying her feelings and as she did, lightbulbs started going on. She said:

"I realize that I don't know what I am feeling because I ignore my feelings. All of my energy has been going into keeping my husband and my children happy."

Karen realized that once she married, she stopped being herself. She had given up her own interests and focused on the needs of her family.

Before therapy, all of this felt normal to Karen. The more she thought about it, the more she could connect the dots. In her family of origin, her feelings hadn't been appreciated. She realized she had learned to keep them to herself, so as not to make waves. As soon as she got married, she fell right back into this pattern.

Are you like Karen? Do you have little awareness of your own feelings and needs? Or do you just ignore them in order to not make waves?

If your identity is measured by keeping others happy and being what others want you to be, what use is it to know how you feel? For me, with my therapist, the invisible force of my intimacy style was pushing me to accommodate and not disappoint him. I also didn't feel like it was my place to ask him what he was doing.

If I was a "good client," I would let him work in the way that felt best to him. Never mind how that felt to me.

I'm not saying I was consciously aware of these thoughts. And I bet they were there. Had it been a less experienced therapist, I suspect my rationale would have something like,

"Oh, he's new and maybe nervous. I don't want him to feel bad about how he's doing so I won't say anything."

Have you felt this way in relationships? Have you blindly focused on others with no awareness of your needs?

This experience with my therapist wasn't an enormous deal in my life. I do wish he would have helped me figure out where this pattern came from and how to change it. And in the scheme of things, letting him work on his plants while I felt ignored didn't have huge consequences.

And what if, instead of a therapist, he was a friend who wanted me to do drugs when I really didn't want to? Or have sex?

the ramifications of appeasing can be serious

As a client tearfully shared with me:

"When I was a teenager, I got myself into some bad situations. I guess, if I am truthful, it was assault. I was just too nervous to speak up. I was scared that if I tried to stop it or said no that the guy would tell other people, and no one would like me. So, I never told anyone."

I have cried silent tears on so many occasions as I have listened to similar stories. Tearful, embarrassing accounts of unwanted sexual experiences because of feeling uncomfortable saying no. Or sexual assaults never spoken of, for fear of what others would think.

I have witnessed and listened to countless women share ways

in which they have worked hard trying to keep the people in their lives happy, meanwhile falling deeper into exhaustion, anxiety, and depression.

Those experiences fuel the passion driving me to write this book. Before ending this chapter, I want to take a moment to talk about appeasing that developed during childhood as a way of trying to stay safe.

children are resourceful

Children can develop the strategy of attempting to keep people happy as a way of trying to keep the peace or stay safe in scary situations. Let's take a moment to look at how this might develop or show up.

Sally was a caring and intelligent woman who came to see me for help in navigating a new relationship. As we explored her interactions, we noticed how much she focused on making sure her new male friend had what he needed. Since Sally had two sons, initially, this seemed to be her maternal instincts at play.

As our work progressed, she shared that her mother had narcissistic tendencies. Sally had learned that things went more smoothly for her if she kept her mother happy. She became quite adept at anticipating her mother's needs. It surprised her to realize that she carried this pattern into all of her relationships.

For Sally, this learned strategy was about avoiding her mother's criticism. For others, the consequences of not anticipating family members' needs can feel like, or be, a matter of life and death.

In families where violence is common, children often attempt to manage the situation by trying to keep the violent person happy. When these children grow up, this pattern of trying to keep others happy can show up as the default way of interacting in relationships.

For women who developed this style of relating in violent families, trying to change these patterns can bring up significant fear of danger. If you are a woman with a history of trauma or violence, the unraveling of these patterns will likely connect you with old memories that may very well be scary. Please consider reaching out for professional support. A therapist can help you safely work through these memories.

I will talk much more about appeasing after we talk about disconnecting.

in a nutshell

- The pull to appease is at the core of an entangled intimacy style.

- When I am appeasing, my focus is on you and your needs.

- Love is defined by how well I please you and keep you happy. How well I do this also determines my sense of being "okay."

- You may have learned this style of relating from the women who came before you, or you may have developed this pattern as a child in an effort to stay safe or to keep the peace.

- Most women realize these beliefs are unreasonable, and there is a powerful pull to do it anyway. Despite what you may believe this has less to do with your strength as a woman, and more to do with the way our brains work.

- Repeated behaviors become automatic, "default networks" in the brain. This means they can easily be repeated and can be triggered without our conscious awareness or direction.

- Safety is a priority for the brain and so connections related to safety become wired in a sturdy way.

- Because of this, fear often comes up when you try to change them.

ideas for reflection

- In thinking about your early relationships, what did you learn about love and connection?
- What does it mean to love someone, and how does that person know that you love them?
- How might the pull to appease be impacting your life?
- If you don't relate to the tendency to appease, does the thought of it bring up any fear?

chapter five
disconnecting

Disconnecting is just as it sounds. A disconnection happens between people. I am no longer concerned or aware of how you are feeling or what you might need. Or I might be aware of what you want or need, and I no longer care because I have had it with trying to keep you happy, or I believe that I no longer need you.

Disconnecting can happen through distance—by walking out of the room or moving across the country or other times, it occurs through emotional disconnection. Your needs are no longer on my radar.

Remember, in appeasing you are trying to keep the other person happy. You are focused on their needs. In disconnecting, your focus is on getting your needs met without awareness or concern for the needs of those with whom you have disconnected. A simple way of thinking about it is:

Appeasing = focus out;

Disconnecting = focus in.

Disconnecting can either be a learned way of relating to others, or it can happen as a reaction to appeasing. Let's begin by talking about disconnecting as a learned way of relating. After that, we will talk about the disconnecting which happens in reaction to appeasing.

disconnecting as an intimacy style

In this style of relating, family members care about each other, and what they have learned about intimacy is that the emotional lives of others aren't their business or concern.

In this style of relating, someone in the family might have an eating disorder or be severely depressed, and the other family members don't feel it is their place to interfere or get involved. This isn't for a lack of caring. I have had clients say,

"We care about each other; we just don't get into each other's business."

I imagine this intimacy style passes through the generations similarly to the entangled style. I have had far fewer clients with this style of relating, so I have less to share about it.

I bring it up because if you have an entangled style of relating, a relationship with someone with a disconnecting style may lead to misunderstandings, fear, and hurt feelings. Let me share an example with you.

appeasing meets disconnecting

Tamara, a newly married women in her late 20s came to see me for help with her anxiety. As we worked on her anxiety, we realized much of it related to her relationship with her husband. Tamara was afraid—well, maybe terrified is a better word—that he no longer loved her.

Tearfully, she shared that her husband would come home from work and *"just announce that he was going out with friends,"* or on the weekends, he would make plans without even talking to her. I wasn't sure what was happening, and we discovered a big clue after a visit from his family.

Tamara shared that spending time with his family had been a *"nightmare."* She said everyone just *"did their own thing."* People would announce they were off to some place for the day, never asking how that would be for others or whether she had made other plans. She said, *"It was infuriating!"* Tamara couldn't believe they would operate like that. And what was even more difficult to understand was that *"none of them seemed bothered by it."*

To Tamara, expressing her love meant making sure her husband was happy. She was careful to consider his needs and always made sure her plans were okay with him. If he wasn't up for doing something, they wouldn't do it. She had learned an entangled style of relating.

So, when he didn't include her in his planning, it seemed obvious to her that she was no longer important to him. As she shared this and continued to think about the weekend with her husband's family, she had one of those lightbulb moments. She realized that her husband interacted with her *exactly as his family had interacted with each other.*

It wasn't a lack of caring or love; it was a learned family behavior.

And it hurt so much because her view of love meant that he would do it the way she did—he would keep her happy.

They had learned very different things about love and living together. And she had been interpreting his actions through her lens of the entangled intimacy style and as a result felt unloved.

What is important is to realize that some families operate at the other end of the continuum from the entangled side—a style of relating that might be described as disconnected or detached.

Interacting with someone who has a detached style of relating may bring up intense feelings of not being loved or cared about in someone with an entangled intimacy style. So, it is something to keep in mind in understanding your relationships.

Now let's take a moment to talk about the disconnecting that happens in reaction to appeasing.

reactive disconnecting

Do you ever give and give to the point of exhaustion and then say to yourself, or someone else, *"I'm done!"* And you walk away? Maybe you don't walk away; instead, you stop talking or withdraw, emotionally, from the relationship.

Or do you reach a limit and let your partner, friend, or boss have it about all that you have been holding inside? These are examples of the disconnecting that happens in reaction to appeasing.

Getting to this point is inevitable for almost everyone who has this intimacy style. It is just impossible to keep giving and not getting your needs met. Well, not impossible, and the consequences are severe.

Valerie, a client of mine, was caring for her aging mother in addition to her own family. Her physician referred her to me for help with her depression. Valerie wasn't taking care of herself. She spent every moment caring for her family, her mother, and trying to keep her house in order. It exhausted her.

Valerie was someone who didn't swing to disconnecting. She stayed firmly planted on the appeasing side, and her health was suffering.

In my experience working with clients, this is unusual. Most women with this style of relating swing from one side to the other.

there is a limit

You give and give until you can't take it anymore, and then you disconnect in one way or another.

I was meeting with a client today who has been working on her entangled intimacy style for a while now. When she talked about the disconnecting she had done in a relationship, she described it as like a snake striking out. It was such a beautiful description of the "striking out" which often happens in disconnection.

She spoke of how she had been holding and holding in her reactions until they just came out, quickly, like a snake striking. And then just as quickly, she regretted what she said.

disconnecting feels good—until it doesn't

There is something life-affirming about the swing to the disconnecting side. There can be a sense of standing up for yourself. Of taking a stand—of being independent. It can feel freeing.

One of my clients reported feeling *"glee"* when she was disconnecting. Other women have described it as *"feeling strong"* or *"getting to do what I want to do."*

Unfortunately, that feeling is usually short-lived. Most people end up dropping into a low mood afterward. Many feel guilty, and often women feel the need to make amends after lashing out. Or a terrible fear of being alone may surface. Sometimes, there is an enormous sense of loss.

Remember keeping people happy and approving has been wired for safety, so while disconnecting may feel good in the moment, later, it usually evokes fear and guilt.

So, let me back up a bit and talk more about reactive disconnecting.

the swinging pendulum

If we think of the swinging pendulum in an entangled intimacy style, swinging back and forth from side to side, one side would be appeasing, where all my focus is on the needs of others and the other side would be disconnecting. On the disconnecting side, I am finally focusing on my needs, and I have stopped focusing on your needs.

I like the idea of a pendulum because it can't stay on one side. It swings back and forth. Similarly, it is usually difficult to stay on either side in an entangled intimacy style—there is a swing from appeasing to disconnecting and back.

In the beginning, most people are unaware of the tendency to swing from appeasing to disconnecting. In fact, many will say, *"I don't do that,"* only to realize that, yes, they do. It just may not be as dramatic as the examples I am using to illustrate the point. When we look closely at their interactions, the pattern shows up.

Clearly, I still have snakes on my mind and sometimes, disconnecting can be like a snake slithering away in the grass. Or, as one of my clients described it, as *"slipping away."*

In Nancy's case, it was the strike. I will come back to the tendency to slip away.

Nancy

Nancy, a single woman in her 40s came to see me feeling worried about her anger. She shared that she would *"lose it"* with people and that her anger was causing some pretty severe problems in her life.

Nancy longed to be married and to have a family. She said that she always *"blew it"* in relationships by getting angry. This happened in her intimate relationships, as well as at work. Nancy told me in a quiet voice about a reprimand she received for getting angry with her boss.

As Nancy shared her story, I struggled to imagine the woman sitting across from me getting angry. She was polite and thoughtful. She complimented me on my office and brought me her insurance card, even though I had neglected to ask her to do that.

She seemed kind and easy to be around. I struggled to imagine her as the angry person she described in her paperwork. As we began our work together, the pieces started coming together. I realized that Nancy's thoughtfulness and caring were signs of a tendency to appease and not simply thoughtful gestures.

Nancy related that she was highly intuitive and an empath. She said that she could sense how people were feeling and what they needed. She shared that, because she had that knowledge, she worked hard to be sure people got what they needed.

At work, she would notice when her boss was looking stressed and would step in to help. In her romantic relationships, she anticipated her partner's needs. If her partner looked sad, she would do something to "make him happy."

She was proud of these qualities. She believed that keeping people happy *is what you do when you care about someone.*

After a while, in her relationships, she would start to feel resentful. Awareness would build that she was doing most of the giving. This led to resentment and then to anger. Nancy shared with me that in those moments, she would get mad and yell or she would leave. Sometimes, she would shout, *That's it; we are over!*

In that moment, what she was saying felt true. Her needs weren't getting met, and she really believed that she was better off alone, that it wasn't worth it to stay in the relationship. She didn't need it. Later she would feel guilty about her words and actions, and afraid that her boyfriend would leave her because of her anger.

Many times, her fears were realized—the relationships *were* over, leaving Nancy feeling devastated and ashamed. The anger she had been feeling no longer seemed important. She was lonely. Being by herself wasn't what she wanted.

She would vow to do better in the next relationship. She promised herself that she wouldn't get so angry and that she would be more tolerant.

Nancy saw her anger as the problem. She believed it was her anger that was keeping her from getting what she most wanted in life, a loving partner. She was overlooking what led up to the anger.

In Nancy's moments of anger, she could see things clearly. She felt strong and powerful, and she spoke up for herself. What she was saying needed to be said.

The problem was that she spoke up from a place of disconnection—a place where only what she was feeling mattered. She felt entitled to speak her mind, and she did so with little regard for the feelings of her boyfriend or for *how* she said what she said.

As a result, her communications didn't have the results she hoped they would, and her good feelings didn't last very long, being quickly replaced by guilt, fear, or loneliness. This led her to her vow to be more tolerant and right back to appeasing in relationships.

Nancy is a good example of how:

- appeasing leads to disconnecting
- disconnecting feels good in the moment, while later is often seen as the problem
- disconnecting leads right back to appeasing

Have you had experiences like this? Times when you let grievances build up, and when you finally spoke up, you did so with little concern about how your words would come across?

And did it feel good in the moment only to be followed by guilt and fear? Like Nancy, do you believe the problem is your temper or self-control? Because of that, has your confidence plummeted? Do you feel anxious and depressed?

If so, please know that this is not a defect in you! This is a pattern I see over and over in the women who come to see me.

In therapy, as soon as we identify a tendency to appease, I am waiting for disconnecting to show its face. Disconnecting seems to be an automatic response to appeasing.

I really want you to hear that.

disconnecting doesn't have to happen in anger

When I shared the idea of resentment building and then letting someone have it, one of my clients said: *"That's not me. I wouldn't do that."*

When we delved a little deeper, I discovered her tendency was to give until she couldn't give anymore and then *"just slip away."* This seemed to her to be a workable solution until we talked about how she felt about herself for handling it that way. She said,

> *"I think I would have felt better about myself if I had been honest. But it was just never enough, and I had to get away!"*

Slipping away was the only way she knew to get her needs met. I want to say that again because it is important. If you have this intimacy style, *disconnecting is the way you know how to get your needs met.* So, of course, you are going to do it in one form or another, or you'll feel anxious, stuck, and depressed. And like Valerie, your health may suffer.

The problem is that disconnecting doesn't work very well, either. You end up alone or feeling guilty and afraid. Or, like my client, ashamed of how you handle situations. These feelings drive you right back to the appeasing side.

remember, this isn't conscious

Most women with this intimacy style want to do a better job of caring for themselves in relationships. Many come in to see me with "better self-care" as the goal. And when they get close to someone, their default wiring takes over and they feel this powerful, force pulling them to keep the other person happy. Without conscious awareness, these defaults are triggered and lead to them losing themselves in the needs of the other person.

I have this image in my mind of a piece of metal and a magnet. As the metal gets closer to the magnet, there is a force pulling them to connect. Can you imagine that pull between the metal and a magnet? That pull reminds me of the pull to appease in an entangled intimacy style.

Most times, appeasing can't be maintained, and women escape the magnetic pull of appeasing by disconnecting or by moving out of the magnet's range.

Unfortunately, disconnecting isn't comfortable, either. There is guilt and loneliness. And those feelings pull you back toward connection. As soon as you get close, you feel that magnetic pull to keep the other person happy. Have you felt that? Do you feel it in your core?

Are you wondering what to do about it?

If so, hold on tight. We will work on that in part two.

in a nutshell

- In appeasing, the focus is outward—on the needs of others and seeking approval, while in disconnecting, the focus is inward on your own needs with little or no awareness or concern for the needs of others.

- Disconnecting can happen emotionally, through words or behaviors or through physical distance.

- Sometimes disconnecting is a learned way of relating. In this style, people have learned to stay out of each other's emotional lives.

- If you have an entangled style, the behaviors of someone with a disconnected style might seem uncaring or give you a sense of being unloved.

- Disconnecting is most often an automatic reaction to appeasing and typically happens when women have reached their limit.

- Although disconnecting often feels good initially, the sense of freedom is usually short-lived. Disconnecting often leads to guilt, fear, or isolation because the other person's needs haven't been considered.

- Disconnection almost always leads right back to appeasing.

- The pendulum keeps on swinging!

ideas for reflection

- Take a moment to think about the people you know. Have you known anyone who seems to have learned a disconnecting way of relating in relationships?
- If so, what feelings came up for you when interacting with them?
- In what ways do you disconnect in relationships? Do you strike like a snake or slither away?
- What do you experience when you have disconnected? How do you feel?
- Does disconnecting lead you back to appeasing? Think about some examples of this in your life.
- Or have you learned to disconnect as a way of avoiding the pull to appease? If that is the case, take a moment to describe when and how you do this.

If you disconnect to avoid appeasing, you aren't alone. In the next chapter, we'll explore how disconnecting can be a way of avoiding appeasing in the first place.

See you there.

chapter six

disconnecting: the chance to be yourself

Sometimes women don't think they have an entangled style of relating and don't appease, when in fact, they disconnect to avoid appeasing in the first place. Because of this they don't see themselves as having an entangled intimacy style or appeasing tendencies.

Remember that statement that stuck with me from my family therapy textbook? Bowen suggested that adult children who move across the country to be independent may in fact be less differentiated than a young adult who can live next door to his or her parents and be themselves.

From an entangled intimacy style perspective, moving away from parents to be oneself can be seen as disconnecting to avoid appeasing. Beth's experience may help explain what I mean by that.

Beth

Beth, a woman in her 40s, was a member of my women's group. In group, we were identifying whether members tended to "appease" or "disconnect." Beth firmly stated that she was a disconnector and from watching her in the group, I agreed.

Some members of the group clearly worried when other members were in pain and had a hard time holding themselves back from wanting to fix their pain for them.

In contrast, Beth struggled with sharing an emotionally connecting message after another member's emotional work. She seemed lost in her own thoughts. There was a sense of disconnection about her.

Beth came in to do some individual work on her struggles with eating. As we explored her family of origin, Beth shared that her mother had often been critical of her. She related never feeling like she could measure up in her mother's eyes and that she found it easier to simply stay away from her. She said:

> "I don't want to get sucked in. I don't want to color my nails, dye my hair, or wear the latest fashions. That isn't me. When I am around her, I can sense her displeasure with me. I start to feel badly about myself and how I look. She says things like, 'You will never get a man looking like that.' I start to worry that maybe she's right. It is just easier to stay away."

During a moment of emotional work, Beth said:

> "Oh my gosh, I'm not a disconnector, I'm an appeaser. I just disconnect to keep out of all that. When I get too close, I get pulled in."

disconnecting to avoid appeasing

Beth's realization is a great example of the tendency to disconnect after having grown up within an entangled intimacy style. In Beth's case, she disconnected through geographical distance. Other women disconnect by cutting off communication to avoid getting pulled into appeasing.

Disconnecting allows freedom to be yourself. Beth could dress as she wished when she was at home across the country, without worrying about displeasing her mother.

It wasn't because Beth didn't care about her mother. She did. Having grown up with an entangled intimacy style, Beth was skilled at intuiting other people's feelings and taking responsibility for them. She couldn't allow herself to get too close, emotionally or geographically because, as she put it, *"I will get sucked in."*

At a deep unconscious level, Beth felt a pull to keep her mother happy. Beth was unaware of this deep wiring. All of this came up in the therapy work we did together. Beth had such an intense reaction to her mother's views because deep down she believed loving her mother meant agreeing with her.

It may sound silly, and if you have this style of relating, you feel it; sameness equals love. "If you love me, you will see and do things the way I do them." With Beth, the sameness at issue had to do with appearance. Of course, there were other areas of contention such as politics and lifestyle choices. Appearance was just one area in which she knew she disappointed her mother.

And that right there is why sameness is such an important aspect of the entangled intimacy style. How could Beth possibly keep her mother happy if her looks, political views, and lifestyle choices disappointed her? To express her love, she needed to keep her mom happy, which meant having similar views as her mother and changing who she was in the world.

When I have discussed these beliefs with clients, I have often heard comments like,

"But if I disappoint her, how will she know that I love her?"

Caring and keeping people happy become wired so tightly together that in the beginning, it is almost impossible to see them separately. Love just simply feels like it is about keeping people happy. It is what you do when you love someone. It is hard to imagine loving someone *and* them being displeased.

At an emotional level, Beth felt trapped. She believed that if she stayed connected with her mother, she would have to give up who she wanted to be in the world.

Sound similar to my dilemma as a teen? In Beth's case, disconnecting became a learned style of walking through the world. By disconnecting, she could be herself and keep from appeasing in relationships.

This type of disconnecting didn't happen only with her mother. Remember how, in group, Beth struggled to come up with an emotionally connecting message after another member shared? This was her disconnecting stance at work. Unconsciously, her default wiring was keeping her from getting too close emotionally for fear of having to give up herself.

Staying disconnected emotionally wasn't without consequences in her life. Beth didn't have many close friends. She was lonely, and even the thought of forming close friendships brought up anxiety. Instead, she focused on her career and staying fit.

In our work, Beth also made a connection between her feelings of guilt and her overeating. Eating had become a way of numbing the guilt she felt about cutting off connection with her mom. Eating and guilt had become wired together in her brain. I will come back to this idea of two things becoming wired together in the brain.

For Beth, eating provided some distraction, and when the guilt became too much for her to handle, she would reconnect with her mother. Their phone conversations were brief, tense, and most often ended with Beth feeling angry.

She would then spend the evening stewing, thinking about how awful her mother was, and how she just needed to avoid her.

At some later point, guilt would resurface, and the entire cycle would begin again.

Unlike so many women who spend most of their time appeasing others and then disconnecting for relief, Beth spent more time disconnecting in order to feel the freedom to be herself.

the pull to appease

We talked a bit about this in the last chapter and it is so important that I want to mention it again. Remember the pull you feel when metal comes close to a magnet and how that pull might be compared to the pull women feel to appease in an entangled intimacy style?

Beth dealt with that pull by moving across the country. She stayed outside the force of the pull. Many women try to stay close *and* be themselves and end up giving in to the pull. As soon as they get close and connect with how the other person feels, they get sucked in and appease.

Have you done this? Have you been determined to "stick to your guns," and then when you got close to another person you got pulled into their needs and keeping them happy, and before you knew it you had totally forgotten what it was you were going to do?

If you do, this might be a good time to remind you of the force of our default wiring. If you have ever tried to break a habit, you have felt the strength of default wiring. I imagine in trying to change a habit, it felt like a force was pulling you back to the old way, or you might have found yourself right back doing the thing you were trying to change without even realizing it.

I bring this up as a reminder not to be too hard on yourself if you are noticing yourself in these patterns. You are not weak or defective. You simply have some default wiring that is pulling you to repeat these patterns.

Let's look at how this default wiring played out in Margaret's life.

Margaret

Remember Margaret? She came in because of exhaustion, anxiety, and her weight. At almost every session, Margaret shared with me her intention to take time for herself and relax. And it never happened—well, not until she started working on her default wiring and core unreasonable assumptions.

The moment she came home, and her husband started talking

about his diabetes, she immediately started worrying about him. Before she knew it, she was busy straightening up the house. She knew the clutter from the kids was stressful for him. Her plans to take care of herself went right out the window.

If you have this intimacy style, it is very difficult to take care of yourself within a relationship. The pull of your default wiring to keep others happy will trump your needs. If you are identifying with this style, I bet it happens all the time.

This is one of the primary reasons that learning about this invisible force is critical for your self-care and health. If you want to be able to relax and feel less overwhelmed, unless you plan on living by yourself on an island, you are going to have to work on the tendencies of the entangled intimacy style.

in a nutshell

- Those with an entangled intimacy style often disconnect in order to feel free to be themselves.

- This disconnecting might be planned by choosing to live in a different city or state from where your family or significant others live, or it can happen when you are past your limit trying to keep other people happy.

- Sometimes women hang out on the disconnecting side because of a fear of losing themselves in relationships.

- Either way, disconnection is hard to maintain because it almost always leads to loneliness, isolation, or guilt.

- Disconnection provides freedom, and it comes at a cost.

- That cost often pulls women to try and reconnect. As you reconnect, the magnetic pull to appease can sabotage your best efforts to be yourself, or it can send you hightailing it for the other side of the country, or maybe the world!

- This is the swinging of the pendulum—appeasing to disconnecting and right back to appeasing.

- Remember these pulls are simply well traveled pathways in your brain—they don't define you.

ideas for reflection

- Have you been relating to Beth's story? Have you moved far away from your family to be who you want to be in the world? If so, describe what that has been like for you.

- Do you find yourself feeling guilty for being far away? When guilt comes up, what do you do?

- When you are around your family of origin, do you hold on to who you are in the world, or do you simply pretend to be who they want you to be until you are back on your own?

- If you are in a relationship, in what ways do the needs of your partner derail you from your efforts to be yourself or to take time for yourself?

- How might you begin to use the knowledge that these pulls for approval reflect default automatic programming in your brain and not who you are as a person?

chapter seven
speaking up gets wired with fear and guilt

Susie, a woman in her 50s, came to see me for help with her depression. She felt discouraged about her inability to *"keep her mouth shut and to be socially appropriate."* She said she came across *"too strong"* in relationships and felt guilty about upsetting people with her opinions. Susie worried she had self-control issues or that she might be on the autism spectrum because of her lack of social skills.

In talking with her, none of that seemed to fit. Susie was engaging, sensitive, and caring. As so often happens, I couldn't reconcile her description of herself with the person sitting across from me.

When we began our work together, we discovered a great deal of shame. As a child, her mother had told her that *"she said inappropriate things"* and needed to *"control herself."* As we explored this, we realized a couple of things.

First, sharing her feelings in relationships had become wired with shame, and second, she felt terrified of saying the wrong thing and upsetting someone, so she would stay quiet. She told me that she tended to spend time alone as it was *"just easier."*

Of course, it wasn't possible to stay alone all of the time, or to stay quiet when she was with people, and so eventually she would speak up. As soon as she said something, she felt ashamed. Speaking up had become wired or connected in her brain with shame.

Susie's experience illustrates so many aspects of the entangled intimacy style. First, in her experience, we see the early learning of needing to be a certain way to feel good about herself. Susie learned and wired in her brain that staying quiet kept people happy—which of course, was hard to do.

As a result, she disconnected by staying away from relationships to avoid dealing with the shame she felt when she spoke up. Staying away was lonely and hard to maintain and so eventually, she would connect with others. As soon as she spoke up, she felt guilty and pulled away again.

I'm sharing her story because it is one of the ways that speaking up gets wired with shame. Susie felt shame whenever she spoke up. Her wiring told her that to be pleasing she needed to keep her mouth shut. Many other women feel shame when what they say isn't received well. For many of them a major contributing factor in the formation of this type of wiring is timing.

why speaking up backfires in an entangled intimacy style

If you are noticing yourself in this intimacy style and feel pulled to appease in relationships, when do you speak up? Isn't it most often when you have had it—when you are past caring about what the other person thinks because you are past your limits?

And does your sharing come out in the way you would have liked it to? I'm betting no. We don't communicate well when we have swung over to disconnecting. Why?

Because in disconnecting, I no longer care how you are going to feel about my message. I'm past that. I'm over it. I'm ready to be heard or get my needs met. So, I leave you without saying anything or my words and tone are angry and accusing. Do you do this and then later feel regretful about how you handled the situation? If so, you aren't alone.

Let's take a moment to talk about how changes in the body make it difficult to consider the feelings of others when we are past our limits.

When you are past your limits and have swung over to disconnecting, you are most likely in the stress response or what I call tipped or out of emotional balance. When we "tip," the stress hormones limit the abilities of the thinking brain, making the emotional brain more dominant or in charge.

In this part of the brain there is *no ability to consider the consequences of words or actions.* Those abilities come from the thinking brain. When we are in the stress response and the emotional brain is running the show, the focus is on survival or feeling better, with little awareness of the repercussions of our actions. This is an important concept and one that we will come back to throughout the book.

So, if when you have had it, and you find yourself disconnecting and speaking up in a way that later leads to fear, guilt, or embarrassment, I hope this helps you understand why this happens and to realize that speaking without thinking is common in the stress response. This is because of the impact stress hormones have on our ability to think and take perspective.

Unfortunately for women with an entangled intimacy style, actions or words spoken from the disconnecting side often lead to shame and a terrible double-bind.

Shame often shows up because appeasing is deeply wired with identity and self-worth. When I have spoken or acted in a way which didn't consider the feelings of the other person, "I feel wrong" rather than "I have done something wrong." Guilt is about what I have done. Shame is about who I am.

As a result, for women with this style of relating, because speaking up most often happens during disconnection, it becomes wired with shame. This is a big problem for your self-care. And unfortunately, the brain can further compound the problem.

the brain helps us do it again

Remember how the brain makes life easier for us? Things we do repeatedly end up like highways in the brain. The more we do something, the more the brain helps us to do it again in the future.

Your brain also makes a connection between two things that, repeatedly, happen together. Walk up to your car, and you take out your keys. I mentioned this in the last chapter when I shared how eating and guilt had become wired together for Beth. The connection is especially strong if painful emotions are involved.

I'll come back to that in a moment.

Without realizing it, every time you try to get your needs met through disconnecting and end up having a painful experience filled with shame and fear, getting your needs met becomes wired with those emotions. So, in the brain,

speaking up = bad things happen;

taking time for yourself = bad things happen.

Neuroscientists would describe this as "What fires together wires together." The brain connects two things that happen at the same time, and they get wired together. This is why when you walk out to your car, you pull out your keys. Those two actions have become wired together.

There is also a concept in neuroscience called the "negativity bias" of the brain. The brain preferentially remembers anything that has felt uncomfortable or somehow "negative" to us. The brain's primary goal is survival. We wouldn't survive if we forgot about dangerous things. The brain helps us with this by holding on to anything that results in a "negative" emotion and by keeping us alert for similar situations in the future.

I prefer to use the word "painful" rather than "negative", as I worry that labeling feelings as "negative" gives the impression that they are bad. All feelings are good in the sense that they are messengers. We will talk much more about this in part two. I prefer the terms "painful" and "rewarding" to describe feelings.

Let's look at these two brain concepts in a way unrelated to intimacy. If a strange dog attacks and bites you, dogs and fear are likely to get linked together and remembered. Even though you may "know" that all dogs aren't dangerous, your brain will have registered dogs as something to be feared, and you are likely to feel a wave of fear come up when you see an unfamiliar dog.

This is important for our survival. If we, as a species, had to keep relearning that predators were dangerous, we wouldn't have survived. And it is likely that those of our ancestors who were the most alert to danger were the ones who did survive and were able to reproduce—thus passing on a tendency to be alert to danger. This is great news for survival from threats and not such good news in non-life-threatening situations. In Susie's case speaking up and sharing her feelings had become wired with fear and shame.

This was not a thought-out process; the brain had wired these two things together. When one happened, so did the other.

The same had happened for Beth. She was on automatic pilot when she ate when feeling guilty. Guilt had become wired with overeating. As soon as she felt guilty, she was eating.

No thought required!

the fear may already be there

These are examples of how, in an individual, speaking up can become wired with uncomfortable emotions. As I shared in an earlier chapter, I imagine that for women, there is also wiring that has been passed down through the generations connecting fear with speaking up, especially if speaking up comes with the risk of disapproval.

It has not, and continues to not always be safe, for women to disapprove or speak up and you may feel that energy as you contemplate speaking up about something that risks disapproval.

Maybe this is another way this style of relating is "entangled." It is entangled with the larger experience and fears of being female.

in a nutshell

- In the entangled intimacy style, speaking up most often happens in the stress response and when women have disconnected.

- As a result, there is little consideration for how words or actions will be received by the other person.

- Words are often said in anger, or disconnection is created in some other way such as not taking phone calls.

- Because keeping people happy is foundational in this intimacy style, words or actions that displease others often result in shame.

- The brain compounds the problem by wiring together speaking up or taking time for yourself with shame.

ideas for reflection

- When do you speak up about your needs in a relationship? Do you do so before or after you are at your limit?

- If you speak up or take time for yourself from a place of stress or disconnection, how do you feel afterward?

- What examples can you think of in your own life, of a behavior, a thought, or a feeling that have become wired together?

chapter eight

appeasing in other relationships

So far, most of the examples I have shared illustrate appeasing and disconnecting in intimate relationships. Because these relationships involve deep caring or love, they are most likely to trigger our wires related to intimacy. And these patterns of relating can fire up in most relationships. They often fire up in relation to societal standards such as beauty or body size. We will talk more about that in the next chapter.

For now, let's talk about how this intimacy style shows up in other relationships. To do that let's go back to Margaret. Remember Margaret? She came to me because she was feeling overwhelmed and wondering what was wrong with her.

Margaret often expressed sadness that she didn't see her close friends as often as she would have liked or felt that she should. She didn't feel like she had the energy for it. Not getting together with her friends was one more thing that she felt guilty about.

When we explored this more deeply, Margaret shared that when she was with her friends, she rarely talked much about herself. When I asked her more about this, she said,

"My friends have so much going on. I hate to add more to their plate, so I do my best to listen and support them."

No wonder she didn't feel like she had the energy for it! Margaret was caring for her two teenagers and a husband with diabetes and a heart condition. She was already exhausted. Seeing her friends triggered the same need to care for them and keep them happy that happened with her family. Yet, avoiding them was also draining her through her guilt.

Margaret felt trapped. And as was the case with Beth, food provided comfort when none was coming to her from those in her life.

appeasing at work

Vicky, a professional woman, came to see me for help with anxiety. She worked in a busy office and said that her anxiety was causing her to come home most days with a tension headache and an upset stomach. Vicky shared that she was very perceptive and had always been that way. She said,

"When I was young, I could tell when Mom had a rough day at work. When that happened, I would try to help her get dinner and by doing the dishes."

Vicky related how happy her mom had been to have her around

to help. She went on to say:

> *"I try to do the same thing, now, at work. I notice what needs to be done and just do it. I don't wait to be told."*

When I asked about her anxiety, she said that she is always worried that she has missed something. *"Maybe there was more I could have done."*

Vicky said that she watched her boss carefully and took her cues from her boss's mood. Sometimes her boss seemed irritated, and on those days, she felt especially anxious. She was sure she had *"upset her boss or that she had missed something."*

As we talked more in-depth about Vicky's relationship with her mother, we discovered she had learned an entangled style of relating. Noticing her mother's moods had paid off with lots of positive attention. When Vicky failed to notice or had something else to do, especially as she got older, her mother often withdrew her attention or from the perspective of an entangled intimacy style, she disconnected.

This left Vicky worrying and trying to figure out what she had done to upset her mother. These patterns became her defaults in relationships and were now operating with her boss.

Madeline

Madeline was an office manager and supervised the workings of a busy office. She also had three little ones at home.

She initially came to me because she struggled with anxiety. As soon as we started talking about appeasing and disconnecting, she saw herself clearly in appeasing.

Madeline struggled with appeasing with her employees. For instance, an employee would tell her about her struggles at home, and Madeline would feel the woman's pain; her heart would go out to her.

When this happened, Madeline lost track of her own needs and her responsibilities as the office manager to make sure the office work got done. Madeline would give her employee a break and then spend her weekends doing the necessary work to meet deadlines.

Her employees loved her. And I can tell you, Madeline was very lovable. She generated warmth and caring. And all of that caring was taking a toll on her and her family. Madeline couldn't figure out what to do. She honestly cared about her employees.

How could she not help them out when they needed help?

We will come back to Madeline in part two, so you can find out what she did to change her situation.

appeasing vs doing good work

This morning a client shared with me how stressed she has been at work. She said *"I've been working on my desire to keep people happy and it's different at work. I have to keep people happy at work—my job depends on it!"*

I asked her whether she needed to keep people happy or whether she needed to do a good job. She was quiet and I could tell that she was having a hard time answering. I suspected she was having difficulty answering because in her mind doing a good job is defined by her supervisor being happy with her.

Intellectually she knew that, right now, her boss is very stressed out and generally unhappy—that her "snappiness" isn't personal. And at an emotional level it was a different story. When her boss snapped it felt personal and she immediately felt stressed and afraid. She believed her boss's reaction meant her work was unsatisfactory or that she was not being "good enough." Her stress sky-rocketed because she believed her job was in jeopardy.

As we talked about it, she began to calm down and started to realize that her boss's mood wasn't personal or related to her performance.

Thinking about my client's fears, it is important to remember that appeasing has been so strongly connected with safety in our history as women, that a less than positive reaction from a supervisor can easily be seen as an indication of poor performance and result in fear, stress and a lack of confidence.

Not separating the old tendency to appease from doing good work can hold women back from taking risks, trying new things and advancing in their careers.

appeasing with people in power

Appeasing can be very tricky to detect. Sometimes it is obvious, and many times it isn't. Wires related to appeasing or disconnecting are often hidden beneath other reactions. Tammy's reaction to her health care provider is a great example of this.

Tammy

Tammy, a married woman with two teenage children, initially came to see me for help with her depression and her weight. Tammy had been overweight for the majority of her life and had experienced a great deal of shame around her size. At some point in our work together, Tammy met with a new health care provider who made suggestions for losing weight.

Tammy was surprised by how furious she felt in reaction to the comments. She suspected that old shame wires had been triggered and that her shame had turned into anger and rebellion. We did some processing of her reactions, and we were both surprised by what came out of it. Here is what Tammy discovered.

"When she made suggestions about how to lose weight, I felt like I had to do them, and I had to do them perfectly to keep her happy. I don't think I can do what she is suggesting, and because it feels like I have to do them to keep her happy it feels like a stranglehold and like I am trapped."

We were both surprised. She felt the powerful urge to appease and keep her provider happy, at the same time she didn't think she could follow through with the suggestions—so she felt trapped. She wasn't feeling shame and rebelling about being told what to do, which was our first guess. She felt angry and trapped.

After realizing this and relaxing she said:

"They are only suggestions. It is my body and I get to choose. Even if she is disappointed with me, it is my body and my choice."

This gave Tammy the freedom to consider the suggestions without feeling trapped. Tammy's reactions are a great example of how wires related to approval can masquerade as something else.

does appeasing happen in every relationship?

I would say the answer to this is yes, and the degree and how and when it shows up depends on the person.

Margaret appeased in most relationships. Even at the grocery store checkout counter, she worried about the stress she might cause the clerk by having so many items or having them in such a mixed-up order.

In contrast, Sally said that unless she cared about the other person, or they were important in her life, she rarely felt the urge to make sure they were happy, nor did she feel derailed if they disapproved.

Sometimes, women don't identify with appeasing or the idea of trying to keep people happy and yet are totally derailed when someone disapproves of them. Or sometimes, like Beth, women disconnect to avoid the pull to keep people happy or appease.

in a nutshell

- Entangled intimacy wires are most likely to show up and be felt more intensely in intimate relationships or relationships in which there is some degree of caring.

- And many women with this style of relating are caring women, so these wires light up with just about everyone.

- Appeasing can be difficult to detect as it is often hidden under other reactions.

- Work is one of the places that a tendency to appease is likely to show up. Appeasing is not the same thing as doing a "good job."

- Appeasing can leave you feeling trapped when keeping someone happy goes against what you know is good for you. This is especially true if that other person is someone in a position of power like a physician, nutritionist, and yes, a psychologist.

- Sometimes women don't identify with appeasing and are derailed by disapproval.

ideas for reflection

- In what relationships do you feel the pull to appease?
- Does this happen only with people you care about, or do you find yourself trying to keep everyone happy?
- If you don't work hard to keep people happy what happens for you when you sense that someone is displeased with you?
- Think about whether there are times when you tend to keep yourself at a distance, so you don't feel the pull to appease. If so, in what types of situations or relationships does this happen?

chapter nine
self-worth gets tangled with approval

We have really been talking about this all along, and I'm imagining that you now have a pretty good idea of how self-worth gets tangled up with approval for anyone with this intimacy style.

And before we move into part two and the BLOOM model, let's circle back and spend some time talking about the ways self-worth can get tangled with approval for those with this style of relating.

At its core, an entangled intimacy style keeps us relying on the approval of others to feel worthwhile. This happens in intimate relationships, and it can show up in all types of relationships, as I shared with you in the last chapter.

Women with this intimacy style can also feel a strong pull to appease with society in general or with their social group. This might happen with appearance, body size, career choice, or the decision to have children.

If you have an entangled intimacy style, you may compare yourself to others on social media or within your social group. You may struggle with the strong opinions of family members or spouses regarding your appearance. Or you might ignore personal passions and instead choose a career that family or friends will understand and support.

Maybe you have shared the experience of many young mothers believing there was something wrong with them because their experience of motherhood didn't match what they believed it should be. Or in their words:

"What is wrong with me? I'm not filled with joy being a mother. I love my kids—don't get me wrong. And I hate sitting around on the floor playing games all day. I look at all these other women who love doing that. I should be loving this, and I'm not. I'm embarrassed to even say it out loud, and all I want to do is go back to work."

Or maybe you walk through your days feeling ashamed of your body and believe that accepting and loving yourself is out of the question because your body is too large. Maybe you relate to Olivia.

Olivia

Olivia hated her body. It was too big—she "felt" fat. She felt embarrassed to go outside. She "knew" people were judging her, and so she stayed inside. Staying inside might have been okay, except Olivia was an athlete. She was a downhill skier and rode her bike up the sides of mountains.

She believed she wasn't good enough because her body wasn't

thin. These feelings/beliefs kept her from doing the things she most loved in the world. They left her depressed and lonely.

One of the major problems with looking outside of yourself for approval is that it can leave you feeling isolated and vulnerable.

approval from the outside leaves you vulnerable

Looking outside of yourself for approval and to measure how well you are doing keeps you vulnerable in a constantly changing world. What might seem "good enough" one day can easily not measure up the next. One moment you think you are a great mom after your husband praises you on your parenting abilities, and the next day your confidence plummets as he asks you why in the world you handled a situation the way you did.

If you are "okay" and "good" when you keep people happy, your sense of safety and security rests in something you have little control over. No matter how hard we try, we can't control other people's feelings. We can't be sure that what we do will "make them happy."

We just can't control nor predict how others are going to feel. As my client realized, you may fix a wonderful dinner hoping to please your husband, and your husband may come home after a rough day and have no interest in eating.

If pleasing others determines how well you are doing and therefore your sense of safety, there is always something to worry about. My client Pamela's struggles are a good example of this.

Pamela

Pamela exemplifies how hard it is to "get there" if your worth is coming from approval. In looking at Pamela, you would think that she had it all. She looked healthy. She had a great smile, two adorable children, and a gorgeous house in a great neighborhood. She had many friends and was quite athletic.

On the inside, it was a different story. Pamela lived with constant anxiety. She worried about whether she would maintain her weight. She worried she should be doing more in the community. She was concerned that people were judging her because of her family's money. Pamela worked hard to be what she thought was expected of her—what would keep others happy.

This was a nightmare for her. She could never relax. She constantly worried that something would go wrong, that she would forget something, and that things would fall apart. Her safety and security were coming from things she couldn't control—the reactions of others. Even if they were happy with her now, she constantly worried that would change.

You may find it hard to relate to Pamela and be thinking that your life is nothing like hers. Maybe you are overweight, or you don't have a gorgeous home or adorable children. As a result, her struggles may seem silly to you. You may be thinking, *"Why is she worrying? Get a grip, woman!"*

And I'm hoping you see how striving, and even achieving approval from others may not bring the peace you hope for and instead can lead to a constant struggle to maintain what you have or have done.

Pamela appeared to have it all and yet on the inside nothing felt secure or safe. There was no secure foundation. If who you are as a person and your worth depends on how well you do something or how well you meet someone else's expectations, you will be extremely vulnerable.

Even if what I am doing today is making you happy, what if it doesn't work or I can't keep up with it tomorrow? What if I gain weight or gain back the weight that I lost, and you no longer want to be with me? What if I can't keep up this pace at work, and you are no longer pleased with me?

Have you felt that vulnerability? Is that what keeps you trying so hard?

it's never enough

Are you beginning to understand why it feels like everything you do is never enough? That you are never enough?

If your measuring stick is approval, you are never quite there or secure that you can stay there, so you have to keep at it—working hard to try and keep everyone happy with you.

How can you possibly get to your dream of feeling good enough, being on top of things and having time for yourself? I think you know that it's impossible. You have already tried, and it hasn't been working.

To get there, you are going to have to work on this pattern of relating that is keeping you looking outside yourself for the measure of your worth.

but I do care what people think

I wonder if fear comes up when you think about separating you worth from approval. Is there is a part of you that isn't quite sure? Are you afraid that I am asking you to turn into an uncaring person and move through the world not giving a hoot what anyone thinks and totally doing your own thing? And does that sound terrifying? Maybe freeing—and mostly terrifying?

If so, no, that is not what I am suggesting. When you no longer care what others think, you have swung over to disconnecting.

Caring what others think and feel is natural and healthy. And letting their approval determine your worth—not so much.

The goal is to have your self-worth rest on a solid inner foundation rather than the shaky foundation of approval.

it's right inside

When I bring up the idea of connecting with one's own internal wisdom and strength, most women like the sound of it and either struggle with imagining it is there or feel afraid to trust themselves, especially if others disapprove.

Addressing those concerns is the focus of the BLOOM model. I will share with you steps for learning how to connect with your inner wisdom and how to deal with fears that come up around disappointing others.

Before we move on to the model, in the next chapter, I will introduce you to the idea of being in the middle—the place where you can hold onto your needs, as well as the needs of others.

in a nutshell

- The entangled intimacy style links self-worth with approval.
- The pull for approval can happen in every aspect of your life.
- It can leave you feeling vulnerable in a constantly changing world.
- It is natural to care about what others think of us. When we stop caring what people think we are disconnecting.
- Seeking approval outside of yourself can leave you feeling vulnerable and constantly scrambling to be "okay."
- Connecting with your own internal strength and wisdom can help you build a more solid and reliable foundation.

ideas for reflection

- Spend some time thinking about the ways the beliefs of an entangled intimacy style have pulled you to look outside of yourself to determine your worth.

- In what ways does looking outside of yourself for your worth impact your sense of security?
- What comes up when you think about separating your self-worth from the reactions of others?

part two
the BLOOM model

chapter ten
the mysterious middle

If you think about the pendulum of a big old clock that is coming to a stop, the resting point is in the middle. It will swing back and forth for a while, and eventually it will stop in the middle.

Coming to rest in the middle is what we are shooting for in working with an entangled intimacy style. The goal is to spend less time at either side—or swinging back and forth between appeasing and disconnecting. The middle is the place that holds both your needs and respect for the needs of others.

the mysterious middle

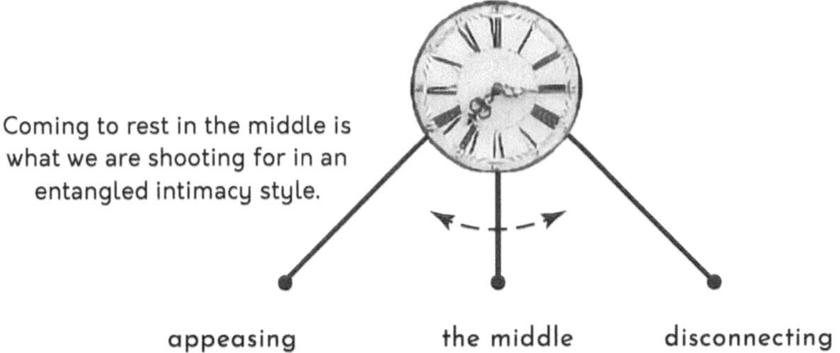

I describe it as the "mysterious middle" because, over and over again, clients ask, *"What is the middle again? And how do I get there?"*

Being in the middle is hard for most people, and for those of us with an entangled intimacy style, the middle is especially elusive. Why? Because the strong unconscious wires of this intimacy style keep us focusing outward on the needs of others and trying to either gain approval or avoid disapproval.

When we have had enough with trying to please we tend to swing right over to the disconnecting side—believing we no longer need the other person and that we need to take care of ourselves. Because of this there is often little awareness of the place in between those two sides—the middle.

what is the middle?

The middle is the place where I'm connected with my needs, and I am also aware of and respect the needs of others. It is the place of "both/and."

In appeasing, my focus is on you and your needs, and in disconnecting, my focus is only on my needs. The middle holds them both.

One way of thinking about the middle is the idea of keeping both "wheels" in a relationship turning—with the wheels representing the feelings and needs of each person. One wheel would represent you and the other might be another person, your family, your social network, or societal standards.

the two-wheeled cart

Over the years, as I've talked with clients about "keeping both wheels turning," one of my clients suggested the image of a two-wheeled cart. This image has turned out to be a great way for others to visualize being in the middle.

The reason it has turned out to be such a great example is because in some ways, a relationship is like a two-wheeled cart. For a two-wheeled cart to be functional, each wheel must be on its own side of the cart and be able to move.

Likewise, for a relationship to be healthy and thrive, each person's needs must be recognized, there must be the opportunity to move forward—or blossom and grow and the partners must stay connected. The wheels must stay on the cart, have the ability to turn, and have some distance between them.

If I am appeasing, I have left the wheel of my needs and am over on your side of the cart trying to be sure you are okay and that I have your approval. A cart with only one moving wheel isn't going anywhere.

If I am disconnecting, I have left my wheel and moved away from the cart. Again, the cart isn't going to move.

For the cart—or relationship—to move forward, the wheels need to be separate (one on each side) and close (they are both on the cart).

separate and close

What does separate and close mean in a relationship? It means that I am not over on your side making sure that you are okay while ignoring my own needs.

It means I am aware of how I feel and what I need, and I haven't disconnected. I am still considering and respecting your perspectives, how you might be feeling, and what you may need.

Each person's feelings and needs are recognized and considered. I may not agree with you, and I maintain connection so that you know I care even if I disagree. This is what I mean by the "both/ and." I am connected with my needs, and I still care about your needs. There is an openness in my heart toward you and your needs while still holding on to my needs.

Maintaining both is usually very difficult. Why? Because of the magnetic pull to appease. If you have this intimacy style, there is going to be an unconscious pull to focus on the other person while ignoring yourself. As the women with this intimacy style have said, *"That is what you do if you care about someone."*

To be clear, I am not talking about never putting other's needs ahead of yours. At times, the other person's needs will take precedence over yours. It is a part of the give and take of a relationship. Likewise, it is very appropriate for parents to put the needs of their children ahead of theirs. And if you are always putting other's needs ahead of your own, your health or well-being is going to suffer.

We need to get your wheel turning and on your side of the cart so that your feelings and needs will be back in the picture and you will have the chance to take care of yourself—to relax, blossom, and bloom.

Let's look at how Margaret worked on this.

how Margaret learned about the middle

Margaret had great intentions when it came to taking time to relax and every time she looked at her husband, she would start worrying about his diabetes or his heart and she just couldn't relax. This was her default wiring in action.

After learning about the entangled intimacy style, Margaret recognized that appeasing was her pattern in relationships and that she had merged in her relationship with her husband. Or another way of saying this is that her needs had gotten lost in his.

She understood that she needed to do things differently if she was ever going to feel less overwhelmed and anxious. And, as I mentioned in an earlier chapter, even thinking about doing it differently brought up an enormous amount of fear for her. She was afraid that her husband's heart condition would worsen, and there was a much deeper fear:

"If I disappoint him or let him down, I'm not a "good" person—he won't love me, and I will be alone."

Cognitively, she knew, this made little sense. And, she couldn't say "I'm a good person even if he feels disappointed with me" without feeling terrified. At a deep unconscious level disappointing others meant abandonment. Because of this, we knew we had to start slowly. The emotional brain would not be quick to let go of anything connected with keeping her safe. She couldn't just "think her way" out of this.

In the same way a person badly bitten by a dog might find it hard to talk themselves out of their fear, Margaret couldn't talk herself out of feeling this way. So, we started with baby steps.

Remember, in this intimacy style, "If I care about you, I will feel like you do." Care and feeling similarly are wired together. So, Margaret started working on deconstructing that wire. She did this by noticing what she was feeling, and then, in that same moment, noticing how her husband was feeling. She noticed that many, if not most times, the feelings they each were experiencing were different.

When she noticed that difference, she also noticed that nothing had changed in their relationship. The level of caring was the same despite their differences.

You may be wondering how this exercise helped Margaret feel more secure and to separate her worth from the approval of others. Before she could separate her worth from approval, she had to deconstruct the old wiring, which was leading her to believe that sameness equals caring or love. Realizing that feeling the same didn't equal love was the first step in helping her to stay on her side of the cart—aware of what she was feeling and needing while still being aware of her husband and his needs.

Although at the time, we weren't sure where this would go, her practicing noticing what she was feeling, while at the same time noticing what her husband was feeling, ended up leading to big shifts in her relationship—shifts that she couldn't have imagined were possible.

There were more steps that Margaret needed to take, and over the years, she has contacted me to share how much her relationship with her husband has changed for the better. Stay tuned, and I will tell you more about that in a later chapter.

Before we move on to what it takes to be in the middle, I want to talk a bit about being in the middle when it comes to societal expectations.

the middle with society

One of the consequences of this entangled intimacy style is that we often appease with societal standards, as well. We strive to be good enough when it comes to the myriad of societal expectations placed on women. This pull to be good enough can also lead to disconnecting when we sense we might be judged, disappoint, or not be seen in a positive light. Can you think of ways that you do this? Most of us can.

Do you work hard to be sure that your body is acceptable?

If everyone is laughing at something you don't find funny, do you just laugh along with them?

If other women are gossiping, do you join in for fear of being the target of future gossip?

Do you compare your parenting with that of others and end up feeling guilty or afraid?

Do you avoid going to parties because you are shy and might embarrass yourself?

Do you avoid bright colors or fashionable clothes because you are overweight and believe you shouldn't dress that way?

Do you avoid going to the beach because others might judge your body?

Each of these behaviors are examples of either appeasing or disconnecting in society or with groups of people.

self-care requires the middle

Can you see how one wheel is missing in the examples that I just shared? If I avoid going to the beach because you might judge my body, I am no longer considering my rights or desires to go to the beach. My wheel is no longer turning on the cart. I am only considering how you will feel about my body.

To take the best care of myself, both wheels need to be turning. I need to respect your rights and feelings, and my wheel of feelings and needs must be in the picture. I have the right to my feelings, and you have the right to yours, even if you are unhappy with me because of my choices.

This is a hard concept for most women with this intimacy style. It usually brings up a great deal of fear or discomfort. I often hear, *"Oh, I don't think I can do that. It would be too uncomfortable to know people were unhappy with me."* So, if you are having that reaction, please know it is a perfectly normal reaction in the beginning.

Let the thought that you can be okay even if others disagree be like a seed that you are planting. As you work through the steps of the BLOOM model, the skills you will be practicing will be like water and fertilizer to help that seed grow into a new perspective. For now, let's talk a bit more about what it takes to be in the middle.

the middle requires balance

To be in the middle we need to be able to observe what is happening inside of ourselves and have awareness and compassion for the feelings and needs of others. This type of observation can only happen when we are in emotional balance, and the thinking brain is on board. Remember when stress mounts and we tip out of emotional balance, the stress hormones impair the functioning of the thinking brain.

So, another way to think of the middle is a state of emotional and physical balance. It is the experience in your body of safety. You might feel relaxed, or you might feel invigorated and ready to learn, create, or love.

In contrast, when outside of the middle your brain and body are reacting to a real or perceived threat. In this state, systems related to keeping you safe are running the show including the more primitive parts of the brain.

In a professional training, J. Eric Gentry, Ph.D., the author of the book *Forward Facing Trauma Therapy: Healing the Moral Wound*,[47] It beautifully describes the interaction of the brain and the body as well as the interaction between different parts of the brain: *"I am both the rider and the beast."*

The body and the primitive parts of our brain, or the "beast," are all about survival. Information is constantly flowing from the body to the brain, providing information about needs for survival. Early memories, assumptions about self and life, and memories of trauma all impact our perception of a current threat as the brain tries to predict what might happen in the present based on what happened in the past.

The job of the beast is to react and to react quickly rather than to observe or think. Imagine how you might jump at the sound of a loud noise. These quick reactions by the beast are designed to keep us safe. For simplicity, I have been referring to these systems as the emotional brain even though we know the body is actively involved.

The "rider" is the most recently developed part of the brain or the neocortex, which I have been referring to as the thinking brain.

The thinking brain can observe what is happening both inside us and around us. It is also capable of reflecting and putting current information into perspective.

All of this allows this part of the brain to analyze and decide on the best course of action. In the case of that loud noise your thinking brain would help you determine what you need to do about the noise. Do you need to take further action like hide, or simply continue with your day?

Putting them together we have the beast poised to respond to any sign of danger, in order to keep us safe and alive, and the rider with the ability to analyze and direct our course of action.

It is to our advantage to be in the middle and have the rider or the thinking brain in charge unless we are in danger and need to react quickly.

a special place

There are many terms used to describe the state I am calling the middle—the state where the thinking brain is on board and fully functioning. Since you are working to be in the middle to separate your worth from approval and the middle requires emotional balance, for simplicity, I will use the middle to also describe emotional balance. I mention this as you may hear this state described in different terms. For instance, you might hear it described as the Window of Tolerance.[48]

Having the thinking brain fully functional makes the middle a special place for many reasons. For those with this intimacy style, the middle is where we have the best chance of getting our needs met while maintaining relationships. And there are many other advantages of being in the middle.

Since the thinking brain is home to creativity, imagination, self-control, perspective, planning, organizing, compassion, and love, being in the middle and in balance allows all of us to set and work toward goals as well as to feel love and connection in relationships.

the middle is the place of choice

In the middle, we can observe, and we can also choose. When we are not noticing and choosing, our defaults are running the show. The brain is using our previous behaviors or experiences to determine what will happen next. Remember the example of walking up to the car, and out came the keys? Default networks are great as they make us much more efficient. We don't have to think of every step for everything that we do.

The downside comes into play when we want to make a change. If we want to do something in a new way, we need to be aware and pay attention so that we can interrupt this default wiring. And paying attention requires being in the middle with the thinking brain fully functioning.

For instance, if speaking up has been frightening for you, your default wiring will help you avoid speaking up. This will happen automatically. To change this, you are going to need to be aware and notice the fear. By noticing you have the opportunity to react in a new way.

In order to be able to notice, you need to be in the middle. You will be learning how to be in the middle and change these defaults in part two.

in and out of the middle

To help you get a better sense of what the middle looks like let me share an example from my life. Yesterday, we had a huge dumping of heavy, wet snow. While I was out shoveling, anger boiled up in me, and I said to my dog, the only one around to listen, *"I hate this!"* I continued shoveling all the while getting more and more angry and feeling more and more like a victim until I finally stopped for a moment, put the shovel down, and took a breath.

I looked at the snow, and it hit me, *"I love snow. That's crazy, I don't hate this."* My thinking brain had just come back on board. When my thinking brain came back on board, I was able to observe my words and feelings and take perspective. I realized what I had said wasn't accurate.

I was exhausted, and my exhaustion had triggered a stress response in my body. The stress hormones had disabled my thinking brain, making my primitive emotional brain dominant.

My emotional brain had "matched" my feeling alone and not having help with a wire related to survival—the danger of being alone. Remember, the brain is always trying to help us be prepared by matching anything that has been threatening or could be threatening, with what is happening in the present moment—it tries to predict what we need to be concerned about.

My emotional brain perceived a risk of being alone from the sensations in my body and from my thoughts and feelings, and then matched them with wires related to the danger of being alone. If I had truly been alone—say lost in the forest, getting riled up would probably be a good thing, as it would motivate me to act. In this situation, it moved me from simple exhaustion to exhaustion compounded by fear, sadness, and anger—well maybe even a little rage.

In that moment, because of my emotional brain's reaction to the sense of "being all alone," my reaction was big—bigger than it needed to be. I'm imagining that if there had been someone here with me in the house, that in my tipped state, I might have come in and let them have it for not helping me with the snow.

Luckily, I stopped and took a breath which allowed me to notice my reaction. In doing that I was able to bring myself back to the middle and a more reasonable assessment of the situation.

My emotional brain or "beast" reacted to a perceived threat of being alone and the "rider," my thinking brain, calmed the emotional brain by realizing that I wasn't in danger. I wasn't actually alone and could have called for help if I chose to. I was also able to notice that I was tired and needed a break.

By moving to the middle, I saved myself all the pain of feeling the "unfairness of being alone," which would have been added to the hard work I faced in finishing the shoveling.

Can you think of a similar situation? Maybe it was picking up other people's laundry off the floor or having to put all the dishes that others had left on the counter into the dishwasher *before* you could start on supper.

Did you have a moment of frustration or anger when your thoughts or feelings felt "true" but weren't? Maybe something like, "I never get any help" or "I always have to do everything." Words like "always" or "never" are cues that you have tipped out of emotional balance and the emotional brain is running the show.

This part of our brain is very concrete. Things are either good or bad, right, or wrong—I'm all wrong, or you're all wrong. And there is no ability to see a situation as an isolated incident. In this case, "I am always alone and with no help."

This disabling of the thinking brain and the concrete perceptions of the emotional brain are essential to our survival. In situations when our life is in danger, we need to be highly focused on survival. I often use the example of if a lion is chasing me, I need to react quickly.

This would not be the time to be stopping and thinking about whether this is a dangerous lion. Or I think of soldiers at war. I imagine a soldier's life would be in danger if he or she stopped to think about the needs of the enemy during combat. These systems in our brain help us to survive when we are in danger.

In life-or-death situations we need to react quickly, and the more primitive parts of the brain help us do this. Luckily for most of us, the threats we face are not life-threatening and so having the emotional brain running the show isn't all that helpful. Staying tipped and believing I am always alone would have led to a miserable experience shoveling and most likely for the rest of my day.

they will light up

These primitive parts of your brain are constantly surveying your environment for signs of danger. This happens outside of your awareness. When a threat is perceived, your body will gear up to help you meet that threat. As this happens you will tip out of the middle and balance as the more primitive parts of the brain take charge to keep you safe. This is normal and essential to our survival. Another time when you are likely to tip is during times of stress.

When I was shoveling, I was overtired, putting my body into a stress state. When stress mounts, old, unreasonable assumptions about yourself and life are likely to "light up" because the brain will be trying to predict anything that might be of danger in order to help you be prepared. And since these fears are often interconnected, one thing leads to the next when we are tipped.

I might start out being upset about being alone shoveling the snow and before I know it, find myself thinking of all the ways people have let me down. Can you relate? Can you think of a time when you started feeling upset about one thing and soon were upset about multiple things in your life?

This snowballing of old hurts or assumptions about life can lead us further into stress and into what I refer to as the desperate state—a place where we feel compelled to act and can't figure out what to do.

It is going to be essential for you to have an idea of what being tipped looks like for you. You will have a chance to work on this in the "ideas for reflection" section at the end of this chapter. Be sure to take some time with this, as having a "snapshot" of yourself when tipped is going to be essential as you work on changing old faulty wiring. We will talk about how to move out of a tipped state in the following chapters and before we end this chapter, let's talk a bit more about old faulty assumptions.

old faulty assumptions

Old assumptions usually reflect conclusions that were made in childhood before you had the ability to think critically about your experiences and put things in perspective.

By perspective, I mean the ability to look at a situation in the scheme of things or to see the whole picture. We can't do this as children. I gave the example before of a child not being able to throw a ball and deciding they will never be able to throw one. To a child, one mistake can come to define how they see themselves. Let me give you another example.

Imagine a young child failing a test. She knows her parents are stressed because they are building a new home, so she doesn't talk to them about failing the test and her worry that she is "dumb."

The next day in class, she is worried about having failed the test and is a bit distracted when her teacher asks a question. She notices all the other kids have their hands up, and she doesn't know the answer. This experience becomes more evidence that she is "dumb." An assumption or wire related to not being smart, and most likely as a result not good enough, has started to form. I call these "lion wires."

I call them lion wires because they are added to the list of threats her brain will watch out for in order to keep her safe throughout her life. Remember the brain tends to hold onto anything that frightens us and uses it to watch out for anything similar as a way of keeping us safe. In this case, her brain will now be on the lookout for any signs of someone questioning her intelligence, which will most likely be equated with a belief that she is not good enough.

There is also a tendency to "overgeneralize" in the brain; it is better to be safe than sorry. So, throughout this child's life, even a quizzical look could be interpreted as a sign of danger in the brain—an indication that she isn't smart enough or good enough and a stress response will be triggered in order to keep her safe.

These assumptions about self and the world can also be formed in adulthood during high stress or trauma. Being in the middle gives us the best chance of noticing when an old faulty assumption has fired up. We will talk much more about the importance of being in the middle and how to do that as we move into the BLOOM model steps.

in a nutshell

- The middle is the place of "both/and."

- It is the place where you are connected with your needs and respect the needs of others. There is an openness in your heart for both your needs and the needs of the other person.

- A simple way to think of the middle in relationships is by imagining the relationship as being a two-wheeled cart and that you are responsible for one side, or one wheel of that cart.

- If you are over on the other side of the cart making sure that the other person approves of you by appeasing, the cart is not going to move.

- And the cart won't go forward if you take your wheel away from the cart through disconnecting.

- When we have tipped out of emotional balance, we are likely to see the world in a concrete way. Things are either good or bad and there is a tendency to overgeneralize (things never go my way) or to be catastrophic (I will never feel better).

- Being in emotional balance will help you gain perspective (see the grey/the exceptions/to remember times when it hasn't felt this way) and have an awareness of your own needs while also staying aware and connected with the needs of others.

- It is pretty normal for this to sound difficult. It will take some practice and a plan. I'm going to help you with both of those in the next chapters.

ideas for reflection

- What comes up for you when you think about being in the middle in relationships—aware of your feelings and needs as well as those of the other person?

- Take a moment to think of a situation and how you might react to it when you are in the middle with your thinking brain, or "rider," fully engaged and how you might react in that same situation when you are tipped and the "beast" is running the show.

- Look at all the aspects of those experiences and how they might differ. For instance, how would your thinking, feelings, and behaviors be different when you are in the middle versus when you are tipped? How would your body feel?

- In considering the differences you noticed between the two states, what might be some clues you can use to notice that you have tipped out of the middle?

chapter eleven
learning to BLOOM

Now you have a good idea why, as a woman, you may have such a strong pull to seek approval from the outside. And you've learned about the intimacy style that drives the need to please and appease. Now we are going to talk about what you can do about it. Before you will feel safe separating your worth from the approval of others, you are going to need to bring new information into the default wires of the entangled intimacy style that keep you looking outside of yourself for your worth.

To do that, you will need skills to recognize when these defaults are lighting up and ideas for how to bring new information into them. If you are going to stop looking outside of yourself for your worth, you will also need to learn how to deal with feelings that will likely arise when you face disapproval.

You will need to be able to tap in to and trust your own wisdom and to ask effectively for support when you need it, whether that is from friends and loved ones or larger sources of support like the spiritual. In other words, you will need a solid foundation of safety. The BLOOM model is going to help you build that.

In the rest of part two, I am going to walk you, step-by-step, through the BLOOM model. The acronym BLOOM will help you remember the steps.

Each of the letters represents an action or set of actions for you to take.

When you get to "M" you will be at that moment you have been waiting for—your moment!

And for those of you who are feeling fear at even imagining doing things differently, I want to introduce you to the idea of entelechy and your wisest self.

Let's start with entelechy.

entelechy

Entelechy is the idea of realizing your potential. Jean Houston, Ph.D., describes entelechy as "the deep Purpose that guides your becoming."[49] Aristotle (as cited in Houston) used the term to describe "higher guidance and purpose."[50]

According to Houston, there is an entelechy available to guide each of us through our lives.[51] Just as it is the entelechy of an acorn to become an oak tree and it is the entelechy of a rose seed to become a rose, there is an entelechy supporting you to become you, and all that you can be.

Sometimes it is hard to go from using other's opinions as the yardstick for what to do and how to feel, to trusting your own ideas and wisdom. The concept of entelechy may help bridge this gap and may be helpful in starting to believe you deserve to be yourself even if others disapprove.

Realizing that there is an expectation for you to reach your full potential can be helpful in starting to believe that you deserve to be yourself and to take care of yourself.

I encourage you to use the notion of entelechy in whatever way feels responsive to you. You might view it as a reminder that something larger than yourself has a plan for you, or you might simply use it as a concept to remind you that you are meant to be you. Or you could use it as a guiding presence or source of support. Use what feels supportive and matches your belief system.

The important part to remember is that just like an acorn is meant to be an oak tree, you are meant to be yourself—not what someone else thinks you should be. You may have a hard time totally buying this, and I bet there is a part of you that believes it.

your wisest self

Most women know, at least at some level, that they deserve to be themselves. And this knowledge often gets swamped by default wiring, outside influences, and by stress. We will talk much more about how this happens as we move into the steps of the model. For now, I want to encourage you to get to know your wisest self.

If you don't believe you have one, use your imagination to create one. Your wisdom will very likely flow through your imagination.

Take a moment to think about what this part of you might look like? How old is she? What would her tone be like? Would it be a combination of strength and kindness? Would one of those be stronger? What kinds of things would you hope that she would say to you? What would you hope her voice would sound like?

Similar to your entelechy, your wisest self is going to be a valuable resource as you separate your worth from approval. This is the part of you that knows what is best for you—that knows you deserve to be yourself. It is the part of you that can see the big picture—the part of you that is connected with your goals, values, and your wisdom. One of my clients refers to this part of herself as "topline Becky."

For women with an entangled intimacy style, this part often gets ignored, especially when other people are around. Practicing connecting with your wisest self will make it easier to use this resource in moments when you are trying to bring new information into old wires and are feeling stuck.

getting to know your entelechy and your wisest self

For some of you reading this book, your entelechy and wisest self may be one and the same. For others it may be nice to know that there is a resource larger than yourself to turn to in difficult moments. Below is a practice for getting to know your entelechy or your wisest self. Use the exercise in a way that feels responsive to you—either connecting with your wisest self, your entelechy or both.

I would suggest that you record this exercise in your own voice so that you can listen as you practice and not need to keep referring to the text. The goal is to practice it enough times that you are able to quickly connect with your wisest self or your entelechy whenever you might need to do so.

Remember to use this guided imagery in a way that matches your beliefs and values. I adapted the practice for connecting with your entelechy from one I learned in Dr. Houston's course, "Awakening to Your Life's Purpose."[52]

Please note that sometimes, this exercise can bring up strong feelings, especially if you have felt unsupported in your life. If so, be sure to reach out for support from your therapist or a therapist in your area. You don't need to do this alone!

Connecting with your entelechy or wisest self:

Before you begin, try to find a place where you won't be interrupted for a few minutes. Give yourself a moment to settle in. You might take a moment to stretch or to yawn. Sit in a comfortable position and close your eyes. As you do that bring your attention to your breath. As you notice the air moving in and out, see if you can slow your breathing down a bit. Not forcing it . . . just allowing your breath to slow down . . . you might try breathing in to the count of six and out to the count of six. And, if you find your breathing is moving faster than that, see if you can allow it to be right where it is. It's okay to be where you are. If focusing on your breath increases your anxiety see if you can focus on the exhalations rather than the inhalations. You might notice that as you exhale your shoulders drop down and you feel your body letting go as you exhale. Now take a moment to allow an image of your entelechy or your wisest self to appear in any way that is meaningful for you . . . She might look like a wise, loving version of yourself—a self who is connected with you and with the wisdom of the universe, of God or, of the spiritual. Just allow an image to come up, in whatever form it takes. Notice that there is a connection between the two of you. Maybe it is a circle of love that surrounds you both . . . just notice the connection in any way that comes up for you. As you see and feel that connection, realize that she knows all of your struggles, all the ways you don't feel good enough . . . and she loves you just as you are . . . feel the love that is there for you . . . the connection and the acceptance and notice what it feels like to feel so loved and accepted . . . knowing that she is on your side and wants you to be you. Realize, too, that she knows all that is possible for you in this life and wants that for you . . . that her greatest desire is to love and nurture you . . . to encourage you to be yourself and all you can be . . . take a moment to notice how it feels to know she is always there and wanting the best for you . . . Now, switch places with her. See yourself as she sees you—with love, compassion, and promise. If she were to speak to you, what would she say? What would she want you to know? . . . Now, switch places again and notice what it feels like to hear those words. Really allowing them to soak in. Spend as much time as you would like with her . . . feeling her love, wisdom, and encouragement. And know that you can connect with her at any time . . . as she is always there for you. And when you are ready gradually bring your attention back to your surroundings . . . wiggling your toes . . . opening your eyes . . . noticing the chair you are sitting on and the colors that surround you. And notice too, what it is like to come back to your surroundings knowing that your wisest self or your entelechy is always there ready to support you.

As you work on separating your worth from what others think, remember that the universe, God or, however you view the higher intelligence that created you, is supporting you in becoming all that you were meant to be.

Before we move on to the steps, I want to remind you of the power of your imagination.

using your imagination

As you work through the steps of the BLOOM model, I want to encourage you to use the power of your imagination and your intention. The brain and body don't differentiate between what is actually happening and what we are imagining. We can use this to our advantage.

Athletes use this type of mental rehearsal all the time. There are many studies demonstrating the power of using imagination, expectations, and intention to create change. I've already shared a couple of those studies with you, and here are a few more that I hope will inspire you to give it a try.

Remember the participants who imagined playing the piano and changed their brains without touching a key? The same seems to be possible when it comes to increasing muscle strength. Muscle strength has been increased solely using imagination.[53] Imagination has also been used to positively impact physical and emotional well-being.[54]

Even hormone levels have changed as a result of expectations or beliefs. In a study looking at the effect of expectations of fullness on levels of satiety hormones, or the hormones that signal fullness, blood work indicated that these hormones increased simply based on the participant's belief that they had ingested a high calorie shake.

In reality, the shakes weren't high in calories; they had simply been labeled to give the impression that they were high in calories.[55]

Instead of using our imagination to our advantage, most of us use our imagination to our detriment by imagining all the worst-case scenarios over and over again keeping the body in a constant state of stress. If you are like most of us, you are already good at using your imagination—you are simply going to use those same skills to imagine what you want for yourself rather than what you don't want.

For most women one of the biggest problems in learning the skills of the BLOOM model is remembering to use them, especially in the heat of the moment. In the moment, when you need to do things differently your brain is going to automatically use your defaults and before you realize it you will be saying "yes" when you want to say "no" or feeling those familiar feelings of despair when someone disapproves.

Mentally rehearsing the skills in your imagination is a way of getting ahead of the game in changing your responses. By mentally rehearsing you will be prepared when you need to do things differently. And practicing in this way can increase your confidence. In the safety of your imagination, you can control the outcome or see yourself successfully managing difficult situations.

In using your imagination, it is important to have a clear intention for how you want to think, feel, and behave when you have separated your worth from approval. What will that look like and more importantly what will it feel like?

Be clear and specific about what you would be doing, thinking, and feeling. Use as much detail as possible. Work on being in the experience and feeling what it will be like to connect with yourself rather than being an observer watching the experience. According to Lynne McTaggart who wrote *The Intention Experiment: Using Your Thoughts to Change Your Life and Your World,* it is important to put yourself in the experience rather than to see or visualize yourself doing it.[56]

Use all your senses. Really put yourself in that new reality. Give your brain and body the experience of having already done what you are wanting for yourself.

Research suggests that when our thoughts match our feelings or when we are in heart-mind coherence there is more potential for change and growth.[57] Let me share an example of the importance of your feelings matching your thoughts.

In my women's group, after someone did emotional work in group, they would take time to "grind in" the new learning that happened during their work. The grind in process involved standing up and stating the new truth ten times with feeling. I learned this practice from Laurel Mellin, Ph.D.

When women did a grind in and were able to feel the power of what they were saying—to feel the emotion associated with the new awareness or truth, the experience was palpable. Everyone in the group felt the truth and felt moved or changed by the grind in. And these women experienced the most change following that work. In contrast, when a member expressed their grind in without emotion, the energy felt flat—nothing felt different as they stated this new truth. Often fear had resurfaced, and we needed to back up and do more work before it was possible to "feel" the truth of what they were saying. Saying it 100 times wouldn't have made a difference if they didn't feel the truth of what they were saying.

So, as you imagine yourself already having the skills you are working on, make sure to feel the reward that would come from having the skill. Would you be feeling confident—maybe joyful or proud? If so, feel those feelings now as if what you are imagining has already happened.

If you feel clueless about how to even imagine doing things differently, or change brings up fear, the steps in the model will gently move you toward changing this pattern, and each step will help you create a clear intention for you to use in imagining being where you want to be.

the BLOOM steps

Each of the BLOOM steps includes a set of skills with a specific purpose. We will go through each step, in the next five chapters.

"B" is about bringing your attention back to yourself.

"L" reminds you to do that with loving self-acceptance and compassion.

"O" is about observing yourself in the moment. In this step you will learn how to notice what is happening inside and how to determine what you need, while maintaining respect for the needs of others.

The second "O" is for offering. This is the step where you follow through by giving yourself what you need. This includes asking for help when you need it.

"M" stands for moving on to what brings you joy and allows you to bloom.

Ready to bloom?

Let's get started!

in a nutshell

- In part two, we will begin the work of bringing new information into old default networks linking self-worth with the approval of others.

- To separate your worth from the approval of others you will need to:

    - get good at noticing when old default wires light up and at bringing new information into them

    - gain skills to deal with feelings that will inevitably come up when you face disapproval

    - know how to tap into and trust your own wisdom and, be able to ask for support when you need it, whether that is from friends and loved ones or larger sources of support like the spiritual

- In other words, you will need to build a firm foundation of security and support—the BLOOM model will help you do that.

- If you find it scary even thinking about beginning to trust your own wisdom, using your imagination, or connecting

- with your wisest self or your entelechy, may help you get started.

ideas for reflection

- What fears are coming up as you move into part two and begin the work of separating your worth from the approval of others?

- In what ways could you use the concept of entelechy—that just like a rose seed is meant to be a rose, you are meant to be yourself—to support you in separating your worth from the approval of others? Or, if you don't relate to the concept of entelechy, what are your beliefs about who you are meant to be in this world, and how could you use those beliefs to support you in being yourself?

- What did you notice when you connected with your wisest self and/or your entelechy?

- In what ways do you already use your imagination in your life? Think about whether what you imagine calms you or tips you into a stress response.

chapter twelve
"B": bringing your attention back

In this first step, you are going to work on bringing your attention back to yourself and the present moment. Why is this important?

It is important because you are going to need to be aware of your thoughts, feelings, and behaviors in order to bring new information into the old wires that keep you looking outside of yourself for approval.

Most of us spend the majority of our day with little conscious awareness of what we are thinking about or where we are directing our attention. We are most often busy thinking about what happened yesterday or worrying about what might happen in the future. For those of us who learned this style of relating, much of that thinking has to do with how well we are keeping others happy or with how "acceptable" we are.

Thinking or worrying about approval has become a default. It happens automatically without your conscious awareness. In order to change it you are going to need to notice when that circuitry in your brain is operating so that you can bring in new and more useful information.

Paying attention in the present moment is difficult for most people. For my clients the reaction is almost always one of frustration or worry when I bring up the notion mindful attention—most want to be more in the present moment, and they don't believe they can do it. Part of the problem has to do with expectations regarding what it means to be successful with mindfulness. I will come back to that in a few minutes.

What I have noticed over the years is that as women practiced with all of the steps of the model, each of the individual steps became easier. For instance, as women worked on loving self-acceptance, it became easier to bring their attention back to themselves.

So, if you have struggled with bringing your attention back to yourself and the present moment, please don't give up yet. Give yourself a chance to work through the model before deciding it won't work for you.

And remember you can always begin the practicing of bringing your attention back to yourself in the safety of your imagination. We'll talk about the specifics of that later in this chapter.

Before moving on, there is another obstacle that women often face in paying attention to themselves that I want to address and that is the belief that it is selfish to focus on oneself.

isn't paying attention to myself selfish?

If you are worrying that working on this step of the model will lead to selfishness, I want to assure you that becoming selfish or self-centered is not the goal of this work.

Usually, the basis for this fear is the tendency, for those with this intimacy style, to swing over to disconnecting in order to meet their needs. Often that swing to disconnecting is associated with guilt and regret for not having considered the feelings of others. It can feel—and in fact be—selfish.

Because this swing to disconnecting is often the way women with this intimacy style have learned to get their needs met, taking care of oneself and selfish have often been wired together in the brain. As a result, when women think of focusing on themselves or taking care of themselves, they feel selfish.

We want to change that wiring so that checking in and asking for what you need happens in the middle—the place where you are connected with your needs and feel respect for the needs of others.

Margaret's struggles with self-focus

When Margaret was learning this skill, she felt guilty. She believed it was selfish to be focusing on herself. A big part of this was her entangled intimacy style. When she imagined caring for herself, she pictured the disconnecting side, where she no longer cared about the needs of others.

Her guilt also related to her beliefs about what it meant to be a good Christian—to be a good Christian she believed she should put the needs of others ahead of hers.

Margaret struggled with this for quite a while. At some point she realized that God would want her to take care of herself and that giving to the point of making herself sick would not be what God wanted for her.

It took some time, and Margaret got more comfortable bringing her attention back to herself. She would say things like, *"I can't be good to anyone if I am dead tired,"* or *"God would want me to take care of myself."*

put your mask on first

I often remind clients of what flight attendants tell us before the plane departs: to put your own mask on before helping others. We are no good to anyone if we can't breathe! You've got to fill your own tank to keep giving.

The goal of this work is not to turn you into an uncaring person. We are working on separating who you are from what you do and what other people think of you.

When you have separated your worth from approval, then you can decide when and how much to give in a way that supports you rather than depletes you.

Your kindness is a gift to the world. Let's find a way to use it without it using you up. To do that you are first going to need to become aware of how you are feeling and what you need. And to do that you are going to need to interrupt the default wiring keeping you focused on the reactions of others.

mindfulness

Mindfulness or mindfulness meditation is one way of practicing bring your attention back to the present moment and noticing what is happening inside. Many people freak out when I say meditation. I hear things like, *"I've tried that, and I can't do it."* Or *"It stresses me out."* Most often, the reason people feel like they "can't do it" is because they have been trying to have a perfectly calm mind with no inter-rupting thoughts. If this is the goal, you won't be able to do it.

The mind is designed to generate thoughts. We can't and wouldn't want to turn that off. In mindfulness, we are simply working with our attention. There will always be many thoughts bouncing around in our minds. We tend to notice one and start thinking about it. Usually what we grab on to is something that worries us. And we are off and running with worry.

Have you had a thought pop up in the middle of doing some-thing else and suddenly you are down the rabbit hole thinking about that other situation?

And you don't even remember how you got started thinking about it in the first place? And now you have wasted a bunch of time that you really needed? I sure have.

And most times, this happens without any awareness on our part. This is where all the default wiring comes in. We have highways of worry networks, and they are well-traveled with no need for road signs because we have been down them so often.

As I mentioned at the start of this chapter, if you have an entan-gled intimacy style, many of your default networks are going to relate to keeping others happy or to worries about what others think of you.

The practice of mindfulness is going to help you notice when you are operating from a default network. When you can notice what you are paying attention to, you have a choice. Defaults will take you down the same old road.

I forgot to call her back—lions and tigers and bears, oh my!

Here is an example from my life. This morning when I was eating my breakfast, I noticed that I had a nervous feeling in my body. When I checked in, I realized that I was feeling fear and guilt as I thought,

"Oh, my gosh, I totally forgot that I promised to call and reschedule a client! How could I have forgotten that?! I had it written on a note right by my computer."

After fussing for a bit, I went back to my breakfast, and I was still having a bit of difficulty letting go of my slip-up. I had worked with this client for a while and was sure she would understand. Despite that knowledge, my slip-up kept popping up. If I wasn't paying attention, I could have easily grabbed on to the worry and gone down the rabbit hole of,

"What was I thinking! I promised her I would call—the note was right there for me to see. I know she was trying to figure out her schedule, and now I let her down. What is wrong with me that I didn't remember?"

And on and on and on. If I let this go on, it is quite likely that similar to what happened with shoveling, this worry about my mistake will light up a larger worry wire in my emotional brain. Maybe:

"What is wrong with me that I can't remember things?" Or "Maybe she won't see me as competent."

Which could then lead to an even bigger worry like a fear about being good enough. Can you relate? Have you mindlessly latched on to a worry and found yourself caught up in a bigger fear?

I can't stop my brain from generating thoughts, and what I can do is work with my attention. I can work with what I am "grabbing onto." Since it is five a.m. and way too early to call her, when that thought comes up, I can notice it and bring my attention back to the present moment and the task at hand—which happens to be eating my breakfast. This is where many people get hung up. Most say: *"I did that, but the thought came back!"*

And I let them know and want you to know *that is totally normal.* The emotional brain may still be sensing danger, or you may simply be on a default worry wire. You don't need to "make the thoughts go away" or "stop them from coming." If that is your goal, you will fail.

And having the thought come back is actually perfect. It gives you the chance to, once again, work with your attention. To notice the thought and shift your attention back to whatever it is you are focusing on in the moment.

Doing this over and over is what strengthens your ability to notice what is happening in those "real-life" moments when you need to notice and take charge of your thoughts and actions. Each time a thought comes back up and you notice it, it is a "workout" for the part of your brain, that helps you observe yourself and what you are thinking and feeling.

Like how doing squats or pushups in the gym will help with

physical strength in your daily activities, practicing being mindful of your internal world will help you notice in real time when you are deferring to the needs of others or disconnecting to get your needs met.

taking worries seriously

I often have clients express the concern that if they don't pay attention to their worries, they might miss something important—a very legitimate concern.

If a worry keeps coming up, I like to use the following two questions to help me deal with it and avoid spinning in worry.

1. Is there anything *in this moment* that I could do about it?

2. *In this moment,* do I want to do that? "In this moment" is critical to both questions.

Here is the example I have often used with clients to illustrate this practice.

"When I was driving to work this morning, my car was sounding funny, and as I am sitting here with you, I am worrying about it. So, I ask myself, is there anything in this moment that I could do about it? And, yes, I could let you know that I am worried and need to stop our session and go out and see if my car will start. Then I ask myself, do I want to do that? No, that would be ridiculous. I could easily check on it between clients. So, I have now dealt with my worry. I have handled, it, and I can fully bring my attention back to you. If the worry comes up again, I can remind myself that I already have a plan and bring my attention back to our session."

Mindfulness is built right into this tool. I noticed the worry and realized it was distracting me. The tool helped me deal effectively with the worry rather than have it continue to spin in my mind. And taking the worry seriously helped calm the part of me that was worrying my car wouldn't start and that I wouldn't get home.

I often encourage women to imagine themselves helping a child as they move through the steps of this tool. Most women easily come up with how they would help a worried child. They realize that ignoring a child feeling afraid isn't a very effective strategy. A child needs to know that you "hear" them and are going to take care of it. The same goes for your emotional brain.

Women also, intuitively or from experience, know that with a worried child once everything has been done that can be done, it is time for reassurance and redirection—saying something along the lines of, *"We've handled it,"* or *"We've got it. Now let's go . . ."*

We will spend more time talking about how to deal with worries and fears in the "O" chapters.

practicing mindfulness

Practicing with mindfulness is going to be essential in order to get to the place where you can use it to bring your attention back to yourself. And, you don't have to be sitting with your knees crossed to practice. You can build it right into your day—although sitting in quiet meditation certainly is a useful way of practicing.

You can practice being mindful in whatever you are doing. It could be while you are driving, walking, doing the dishes, making your bed, talking with your partner, or taking care of your children.

No matter what you are doing, your attention is likely to wander, and when it does, you have the chance to notice and bring it back to the task at hand.

Brushing your teeth is an easy way to practice. If you are like me, your attention wanders during that task. I am often planning my day rather than focusing on my teeth. So, for me, bringing my attention back and noticing how I am brushing is a good way of practicing mindful attention—and it is also good for my teeth!

How you practice is not as important as regularly practicing. If you want to change the wiring in your brain you are going to have to do things differently. If you are like most of us you already feel overwhelmed and despite this, most women find ways to work something important into their schedule. How would you work it in if someone else needed your help?

connecting with yourself

The BLOOM model is, in essence, a way of connecting and caring for yourself—a practice that will help you notice default wiring connecting worth and approval that needs updating. It will also help you take better care of yourself and tap into your own strength and wisdom.

Having this connection with yourself is going to be essential for dealing with the feelings that are bound to come up when others disagree or disapprove of your choices or of you. It is going to be essential for you to know that you will be there for yourself no matter what. We will talk much more about this in the "L" step of the model. Connecting with yourself will help you keep your finger on the pulse of your inner life so that you can determine what you need rather than being bounced around by the opinions or reactions of others. In learning to connect with yourself, you will be learning how to give yourself some of that love and care that you have been giving to others in your life.

To get started learning the skill of connecting with yourself, you are going to build on the practice of mindfulness. In this step you are going to use mindfulness to bring your attention back to yourself. Once you do that, you are going to spend a few moments giving your body comfort and connecting with the love and support that is available to you in your life from those who love you, from your wisest self, your entelechy, or from the spiritual.

I expect that for some of you even thinking about trying this type of connection with yourself might bring up uncomfortable feelings. If this sounds like you, please know that it is perfectly fine to be right where you are with this.

See if you can allow yourself to be curious. Go into the practice with as few expectations as possible. And as you practice, simply notice, with curiosity, any feelings or reactions that come up. Let anything you notice simply be information—not right or wrong—simply information.

connecting practice—bringing your attention back to yourself

Because connecting with yourself is such an integral part of separating your worth from approval, to make it easier for you, I created a downloadable recording of the connection exercise. This way you can simply relax and listen. You can also carry the recording with you and use it in times of need. You can download the free recording here: bit.ly/Debsgifts4u.

With practice, you will be able to bring to mind the components of this step without using the recorded meditation. The goal is to get to the place where you can do it automatically and quickly. In the beginning, take your time and let yourself notice and feel. For most women, it is helpful to practice with as few distractions as possible. Closing your eyes may also help.

Find a comfortable place where you won't be disturbed for a few moments. Before you sit, take a moment to shake out your body or to do some nice big stretches. You might sigh or hum as you shake out your body. Long exhalations give our nervous system the signal that all is well. Having a relaxed nervous system will help you with this practice. When you are sitting comfortably, imagine that you are pulling yourself out of the river of the busyness of your day... up onto the bank where all of that busyness can float on by... knowing that whatever you have been doing or focusing on will be right there waiting for you when you are finished. You might imagine thoughts as they come up as being like leaves... noticing them coming into your attention and then watching them floating gently down the river... or you might imagine watching them floating by like clouds in the sky. Listen for a moment to the sound of the water as it moves past you... As you do, notice how soothing the water sounds. Take a moment to notice the beauty that surrounds you... maybe there are flowers or ferns or birds singing in the trees... Smell the fragrance of the flowers. Feel the warmth of the sunshine on your shoulders . . . and notice how good it feels. As you feel that warmth, you might notice your shoulders relaxing a bit . . . Maybe they have dropped down some from where you have been holding them . . . if so, notice how good that feels. If not, and a thought, worry, or judgment comes up about that, see if you can just let it travel on down that river . . . knowing that it is okay to be just as you are in this moment. If other worries come up, again see if you can let them float on by . . . knowing that if it is important, it will come back to you. Knowing that right now, there is nothing you need to do; no place you need to be . . . simply enjoy the warmth of the sunshine on your shoulders . . . As you breathe, feel that warmth radiating up into your face, head, and scalp . . . down throughout your body . . . down your arms . . . into your chest . . . your pelvis, hips, and down your legs all the way to your feet . . . right down to your toes . . . Feel it surrounding you on all sides, above and below you. Feel relaxation flowing as the warmth travels throughout your body . . . imagine that warmth as the caring from those who love you, or the energy of the universe or of the spiritual . . . feel it moving throughout your body and feel it supporting your very being . . . And, as you feel that support . . . notice yourself letting go of the need to do and simply allowing yourself the chance to simply be . . . just as you are. Notice how good that feels in your body to be so supported . . . so accepted, and so relaxed. Really soak it in . . . imagine it filling every cell in your body . . . take as long as you would like sitting there in the sun and soaking up all of those calming, relaxing, and supporting feelings . . . knowing you can come back to these feelings at any time by remembering the sunshine on your shoulders. . . And, when you are ready, slowly bring your attention back to the room . . . wiggling *your toes, stretching, and maybe yawning or feeling a slight upturn in your lips as you return your attention to your day.*

how was that?

Did it feel relaxing? Or not so much? If not, no worries. It may simply be a foreign feeling to notice and spend time on yourself. Or you may be bumping up against an old assumption that is getting in the way of you relaxing and paying attention to yourself.

For most women, this step gets more comfortable with practice. Just take your time and go easy on yourself. If it feels scary or uncomfortable, think about how you might step your toe in the water by doing a small part of the practice and gradually adding more. And, if you are feeling overwhelmed by uncomfortable feelings, please reach out for support from your therapist or a mental health professional in your area.

practicing doing things differently

The end goal of this work is for you to use the steps in the BLOOM model with enough frequency so that they become the default or a habit. This will allow you to start tapping into your own wisdom rather than using the old automatic circuitry that keeps you looking outside of yourself for your value.

Because the brain values efficiency and therefore prefers to use what is already there, and as most women have busy lives with many demands, practicing these skills with enough frequency to make them the default can be a bit tricky.

When I was learning these skills, many days I would be getting ready for bed and realize that I hadn't practiced a single time. Sigh. You could be the exception, and I bet you will face that same challenge. In the beginning you are going to need to find something that will help you remember to practice. Pairing is one idea for how to do that.

pairing

Most people find it helps to pair the practice of connecting with themselves with another, already established, routine in their day. For instance, you could practice each time you wash your hands or go to the bathroom. For one of my clients who paired washing her hands with connecting, the mirror in the bathroom reminded her to bring her attention to herself.

Others have used mealtimes or natural breaks in their days. Some clients who are frequently in and out of their car have paired connecting with starting their car. You might take a moment to bring your attention inside before you start your car. Or you could take a moment to connect with yourself before getting out of your car. In her book, *Good Habits, Bad Habits*,[58] Wendy Wood, Ph.D., shares three factors that her research demonstrates help in developing new habits. The factors she found are context, repetition, and reward. Let's take a moment to look at the first two factors.

context

Context is everything around you. It is your environment and everyone in it. It is important to have context which will support your practice. In thinking about when you will connect with yourself, see if you can find a time and place that will support you in stopping for a moment to connect with yourself. Look for a time when there will be less "friction," as Dr. Wood describes it, from your world to keep you from following through.

In the beginning, most women with an entangled intimacy style find it hard to focus inwardly with other people around. So, finding a time and place where you can be alone can make it easier—even if that is in the bathroom. If bathrooms don't feel good, could you go outside? Some women even go into a closet.

Or instead of finding a time and place by yourself, another idea is to involve others in the practice—maybe stopping for a moment of silence before or after meals.

The important part is that you set it up. No matter how motivated you feel right now about doing this, when you go back to your day, it will most likely be "business as usual."

repetition

Repetition is Dr. Wood's second factor. If you want your new behavior to become a habit, you are going to need to repeat it. The more you repeat it, the more likely it will become a habit. Remember the brain creates default wiring for repetitive behaviors. Once that happens, you will no longer need to consciously remind yourself. The goal is to practice this often enough that it becomes a default. Could you start with once and increase it to three times a day?

We will talk about the third factor, reward, in the next chapter.

mentally rehearsing with your imagination

Now that you have a plan for when and where you are going to connect with yourself, take some time to use your imagination and the power of intention to help you put this plan into action.

As we have talked about, your body doesn't distinguish between what you are experiencing and what you are imagining. When you vividly imagine doing something, to your brain and body it is as if you have already done it.

The important part is to put yourself in the experience rather than to see or visualize yourself doing it.[59] Be in the experience of connecting with yourself rather than being an observer watching the experience.

Imagine challenges that you might face in taking time for yourself and experience yourself dealing effectively with them in your imagination so that you will be prepared when they happen in real life.

Feel the rewards that would come from taking a moment to stop, stretch, breathe, and feel supported. You might feel more relaxed, at peace, or secure realizing that you are beginning to be there for yourself.

starting your day with intention

Most of us start off our day by mentally running through what we have on our plate for the day ahead—usually with a sense of foreboding around how we will accomplish all that we need to get done.

Why not use this time when you are using your imagination anyway, to set the intention of connecting with yourself throughout your day and keeping your thumb on the pulse of your internal life? Once you have done that, take a moment to imagine yourself following through on this intention. Remember to feel the rewards of having followed through as you imagine yourself connecting during your day.

If you notice fear coming up as you use your imagination, take a moment to remind yourself that it is okay to be right where you are right now. It means nothing about where you will be.

in a nutshell

- The BLOOM model is, in essence, a way of connecting and caring for yourself.
- The first step of the model—the "B" step, reminds you to bring your attention back to yourself. If you have an entangled intimacy style, your attention is most often on the needs of others. To change your default wiring, you are going to need to be paying attention to what is happening inside.
- Practicing with mindfulness during your day is a great way to increase your awareness of where you are focusing your attention.
- Once you bring your attention back to yourself, you are going to take a moment to relax and feel supported—you will make a connection with yourself.
- The goal is to have connecting become a habit or a default.
- Most women struggle with remembering to connect with themselves. Pairing your connection with something you already do like having a meal or using the restroom will make it easier to remember.
- The more you practice with this, the quicker it will become a habit.

- You might also use your imagination to mentally rehearse connecting with yourself. The body doesn't differentiate between what we are vividly imagining and what is actually happening, and mental rehearsal has been shown by many studies to produce similar changes to actual practice.

- Use your imagination and intention to your benefit in the mornings. Set an intention for connecting with yourself and spend time mentally rehearsing doing this and feeling the rewards of caring for yourself in this way.

- In each of the next chapters, we will build on the skill of bringing your attention back to yourself.

ideas for reflection

- What reactions do you have to bringing your attention back to yourself?

- What feelings came up as you practiced the connecting meditation?

- Where in your day will you add connecting with yourself?

- What will you pair it with? How will you remind yourself to connect?

- What obstacles do you anticipate, or have you encountered, in practicing connecting? How will you navigate these obstacles?

- What did you notice when you used your imagination to mentally rehearse connections with yourself?

- What feelings are coming up as you are paying attention to yourself? Any difficult feelings? How about rewarding feelings?

chapter thirteen
"L": loving acceptance and self-compassion

The purpose of this step is to remind you to be loving, accepting, and compassionate with yourself. Of all the steps, this is the most important. If you do nothing else, work on this step.

Why? Because acceptance and compassion calm the nervous system. When your nervous system is calm, you can think rather than react or operate from old default networks.

If you want to feel less impacted by the reactions or needs of others, being able to calm your nervous system is going to be essential. Doing so will allow you to choose your reactions rather than simply responding in the ways you have always responded. Not only that, acceptance and compassion just plain feel good.

Loving acceptance and compassion can become the reward in your connections with yourself. In her work on habits, Dr. Wood found that behaviors paired with intrinsic rewards were more likely to turn into habits. Intrinsic means coming naturally from what you are doing rather than from something outside yourself like a monetary reward.

Feeling the good feelings that come up when you accept and feel compassion for yourself can grow into a reward that will pull you back to this practice.

And self-acceptance and compassion are always available to you. They can be a constant for you, whereas outside reassurance is iffy. One never knows how others will react.

When I was learning about connecting with myself, I felt some resistance. I wanted support from others. I didn't want to have to give it to myself. Do you relate?

It's funny how things happen. During that same time, the time when I was learning the importance of self-acceptance and reassurance, I did something I felt embarrassed about. What I did was far less important than the lesson that I learned. I learned to trust my inner wisdom about what I needed. Here's how that happened.

After I messed up, I immediately called a good friend who was typically very supportive. I expected her to say, *"It will be okay. Everyone messes up."*

Well, it just so happened that on this day, my friend was in a problem-solving mood, and her response was, *"I'm wondering why you did that?"* or something along those lines. My guilt and panic skyrocketed.

And this is what I learned. I knew better than she did, in that moment, what I needed. The answer was inside of me. It was what they had been telling me all along in my training, and I hadn't believed them—not until that moment.

The universe helped me realize what they were saying was true.

you deserve support

You may be wondering from the example I just shared whether I am suggesting that you don't reach out to friends or loved ones for support.

I want to be clear that I am not suggesting that. You deserve support from those around you. And calming your nervous system will allow you to reach out for support in a way that makes it more likely that you will get the kind of support you need and want.

If I could have taken a moment to calm myself down and connect with what I needed, I could have called my friend and said, *"I'm feeling worried about what I did. Would you have a moment to reassure me it will be okay?"*

That would have given me a much better chance of getting what I needed instead of feeling worse about myself.

adding loving acceptance and self-compassion to your connections

Most of my clients have found it hard to imagine feeling acceptance or compassion for themselves. I'll say more about that in a minute. And before I do, I want to point out that there is a pretty good chance you already have these skills down pat. You just use them with other people and not yourself.

And I bet you know how important these qualities are in relationships. You probably couldn't imagine not being accepting or compassionate with the people you care about in your life. Because of this, you are one step ahead of the game. You are simply going to use the same skills with yourself.

Let's start with self-acceptance.

self-acceptance

Most people, no matter what their intimacy style, struggle with self-acceptance. The biggest concern is usually that acceptance is undeserved. I often hear: *"How could I possibly accept myself when I am this anxious, overwhelmed, depressed, etc.?"*

Most often, this ties in with the other concern of, *"If I accept myself, I will never change."*

It is important to know that self-acceptance isn't about giving up, and it has nothing to do with where you might be tomorrow or a year from now. It is simply about seeing yourself clearly—where you are right now without judgment. I like to think of acceptance as not fighting against the truth of the moment.

There are some big advantages to doing this. First, if you accept where you are, you can take better care of yourself because you will be able to see more clearly what it is you need.

Second, learning self-acceptance is going to be key in separating your worth from the approval of others. If you don't accept yourself, comments and reactions of others are going to have more punch. Feeling upset about where you are is also likely to trigger a stress response and light up your old default wires connecting self-worth with approval from others. And, finally, the stress response isn't conducive to growth and change.

In all these ways, self-acceptance fosters growth and change rather than impeding it. An easy way to get a sense of this is to think of a child trying to learn something and the parent saying, *"What is wrong with you that you can't get this?!!"*

What do you imagine will happen for the child? I'm imagining they might get scared and blank out. It probably wouldn't help the child learn. And imagine the difference it might make and how good it might feel if instead, if the parent said, *"I get it. I can tell this is hard for you. Let's see what we can do."*

When you are connecting with yourself, you want your system to be calm so you can think, observe, and get an accurate picture of what is going on inside, and the care you need. Loving self-acceptance is a great way to do that.

If you come up against resistance to accepting yourself, try going with it by saying something like, "I understand and accept that it is too hard to accept myself right now."

That leads us right into self-compassion.

self-compassion

Self-compassion is the skill of seeing yourself just as you are with kindness, concern, and a willingness to help.[60] Similar to self-acceptance, learning to be compassionate toward yourself is going to be essential as you separate who you are from what others think of you.

Feelings are bound to come up as you do the work of separating your worth from approval. Being able to feel compassion for yourself will help you ride the waves of those feelings.

Similar to self-acceptance, compassion is like a balm for the nervous system. It will help keep your thinking brain active so that you can determine what you really need when someone disapproves rather than what your old wires are telling you that you need. It will also help you stay in the middle—connected with your needs while maintaining connection with others.

Let's go back to the example of a parent with their child, and the parent saying in an angry tone, *"I can't understand why you would struggle with this. It's not that hard!"*

Will the child feel safe enough to share what is hard for them?

I don't think so.

Now, let's take an example related to approval. Let's say a child is being teased at school because of her weight, and her parent says, *"Well, if you would just stop eating desserts maybe you wouldn't be in this situation!"*

Do you cringe imagining a child who is already feeling ashamed hearing that? And isn't that along the lines of what you might say to yourself?

What do you imagine that child needs in that moment? Probably to know that their parent gets it—understands that they are struggling. Right?

So, isn't it possible that is what you need as well?

Take a moment to think of a time when you were struggling and someone let you know they cared and were there for you. Maybe they said caring words, or maybe they simply put their arm around your shoulders or gently stroked your hand. It's soothing, isn't it?

It is wonderful to get caring and compassion from others and that isn't always possible. Sometimes no one is around or those around us may be struggling with their own problems. The good news is that whether compassion comes from someone else or yourself, it has the same calming effect on your nervous system.

A simple way to practice self-compassion is to put your hand on your heart and feel the connection from you to you. Take a moment right now and put your hand over your heart.

What do you notice? Do you notice a sense of connection or maybe your shoulders relaxing a bit? Some clients feel a sense of caring or warmth. And in the beginning, some clients don't feel anything or may even feel tense. I'll share some ideas for that in a moment.

You might try adding some comforting words while having your hand over your heart. If you do, make sure to check and see what happens in your body when you say them to yourself. Use words that help your body to relax. Some examples include:

- I'm here.
- I get it.
- I care.
- I won't leave you.

Try to avoid saying things you wish were true and that you don't believe. Your body won't believe you. And Kelly McGonigal, Ph.D., suggests that when you talk to yourself in the second person or call yourself by your name, it boosts mood and motivation and leads to better follow-through.[61] Considering this, it might be even better to add your name to those statements. For instance, *"Deb, I'm here and I'm not leaving."*

if this brings up resistance

If you have learned that focusing on others means you are a good person, feeling compassion for yourself can be difficult, or it can feel bad or wrong.

If you notice uncomfortable feelings coming up around being kind and compassionate toward yourself or felt nothing when you put your hand on your heart, see if you can start with acceptance for what you are feeling. You might say, "That's where I am right now, and that's okay."

Self-acceptance often leads to self-compassion, and both are good for your nervous system. And if you can't feel self-acceptance or self-compassion, no worries! You may just need to practice.

it's a skill

Remember the structure of the brain changes with what you do, think, and feel. When you learn a new skill, the brain creates new pathways. When you practice the skill, the pathways get stronger until most times you can do it without thinking. Take a moment to think of something you have learned to do that became natural with practice.

Most with this intimacy style don't have the pathways in the brain supporting self-compassion. You are going to need to build them. Learning self-compassion is like learning any other skill. The more you practice, the better you will get. I can say this with confidence because I've seen it happen.

I have had clients adamantly tell me they would never feel self-compassion. Later, in moments of distress, these same clients would turn to self-compassion as their "go-to" for getting back in balance.

So, if it doesn't come naturally to you right now, or you felt nothing when you put your hand on your heart, just keep going through the motions. It may surprise you!

Another way of building self-compassion is through the practice of metta meditation.

metta meditation

Metta, also called a loving-kindness mediation, is a practice that involves expressing good wishes and feeling of kindness toward yourself and others.[62] It is practiced through a series of statements such as, *"May you be safe or may you be happy."*

Typically, the practice starts with feeling kindness and love for yourself, and then extending those feelings outward to others. For those with this intimacy style, I have found that flipping the order is more helpful since feeling compassion for others comes more naturally. Starting there may help you begin to feel compassion for yourself.

Here is an example of how the practice might go.

Bring up an image of someone in your life you find it easy to love and feel kindness toward. If you don't have someone like that in your life, you could bring up an image of a lovable pet or spiritual figure.

Picture that person sitting in front of you. Feel their presence. You might notice that they are smiling at you. Connect with your feelings of care for this person, and as you do that, imagine sending them goodwill and kindness as you repeat the following phrases three times.

May you be safe. May you be peaceful.

May you be kind to yourself.

May you accept yourself just as you are.

Next, bring yourself into that circle of kindness and repeat the following phrases three times

May we be safe.

May we be peaceful.

May we be kind to ourselves.

May we accept ourselves just as we are.

Now focus exclusively on yourself—knowing that you, too, deserve goodwill and kindness and repeat these statements three times.

May I be safe. May I be peaceful.

May I be kind to myself.

May I accept myself just as I am.

If you have trouble bringing yourself into this circle of kindness, you might start with sending love and kindness toward yourself as a child. I will come back to this at the end of the next section.

If a critical voice comes up as you are sending kindness toward yourself, let an image form in your mind of that critical part. What does he or she look like?

See if you can extend loving-kindness toward that critical part of yourself—knowing that part deserves care as well. Even if it doesn't feel that way, she has your best interests at heart.

You can also use different words in the phrases. You might use words like happy, healthy, strong, or at ease. Whatever you wish for yourself and others.

focusing on your younger self

Most of us feel compassion for children. Just looking at their youthful faces most often warms our hearts and brings up feelings of love.

When you look at a picture of yourself when you were young, what do you notice? Most women say things like, *"She's adorable"* or *"So cute."*

And I'll ask, *"How about lovable?"*

The answer is usually yes. If so, and you have found it hard to feel loving acceptance and compassion for yourself, how about starting with sharing those feelings with your young self? Since you are already great at feeling compassion for others, feeling compassion for your younger self may be a good way to begin. You can start this by bringing her into the metta practice.

After you have felt loving-kindness for someone else, bring up an image in your mind's eye of yourself as a little child. If it helps, you could look at a picture of yourself.

Really look at her. Wouldn't you wish the best for this little person? See if you can begin to feel love and acceptance for yourself by noticing how deserving the young you is of that kind of care. Then see if you can bring that little one inside of you—maybe into your heart, and expand your feelings of compassion and kindness to both of you—both of you so deserving of kindness, peace, and acceptance.

I've had clients put a photo of their younger self on their phone. When they used their phone, the photo reminded them to take a moment to feel compassion for her and for themselves.

you feel her pain

If you can't feel compassion for your younger self, it may mean you are merging with her. You are becoming her and feeling her pain or unworthiness rather than looking at her from the loving eyes of an adult who knows and understands her struggles.

If this happens, take a moment to "think" about what she is going through and see if you can understand it. Understanding helps you observe rather than be in her experience. Can you look at her and say, *"I understand"* or *"I get it?"*

If you can't do this, here are a couple more options.

bringing in someone else to feel compassion

If it is just too hard to feel acceptance or compassion for yourself, even the younger version of yourself, could you imagine someone there with you, accepting you and feeling compassion for you?

It could be someone in your life who has consistently been understanding and kind. Or it may a spiritual figure, or your entelechy— the life force propelling you to be you, or the wisest part of yourself. You could even bring in a fictional character. It doesn't matter who it is as long as you can feel kindness and understanding coming from them to you. Many people begin practicing loving acceptance and compassion in this way.

If none of this is working, you may need to take some time to allow your nervous system to move into a relaxed state.

why a relaxed nervous system?

As we have talked about, relaxing your body and nervous system allows your thinking brain to come back into action so that you can observe yourself and feel compassion.

Feeling compassion isn't a part of the body's defense strategies. When we are pulled to run or fight, there is no place for compassion. So, if you are struggling to feel compassion for yourself, taking a moment to relax your body or intentionally activating your thinking brain may be just what you need to feel some acceptance or compassion.

getting your thinking brain on board

If you are having trouble observing and feeling compassion, the following questions may help to get your thinking brain back in action.

When working with your younger self,

- "What are the advantages of being the age I am now versus when I was a child?"
- "What do I know that she doesn't know?"

Or in feeling compassion for yourself,

- "What would I say to a friend or a child if they were feeling like I am feeling right now?"

These questions usually pop people right back into balance. Balance allows for understanding, which often leads right to self-compassion.

If these questions don't help you come back in balance and feel compassion, here are some other ideas for relaxing your nervous system and getting your thinking brain back on board.

relaxing the nervous system

hand on heart

I mentioned this tool earlier and will add it here as well since so many women have found that putting their hand over their heart calms them and brings a sense of peace and security.

Try putting your hand over your heart and be curious about what, if any, shifts you notice.

focusing on your breath

When we are stressed, our breathing most often becomes short and shallow. Because of this, one way to calm your nervous system is to focus on slowing down your breath and breathing fully.

To do this you might imagine that you are blowing up a balloon in your abdomen. It helps to put your hand on your belly so that you can feel your hand rising as you fill the balloon with your inhale and lowering as you exhale.

Another way of using your breath to calm your system is to focus on your exhales. Long exhalations signal the body that all is well, so see if you can make your exhale a little bit longer.

There are many other strategies for using your breath to calm your system. Searching online should help you find the breathing technique that is most helpful for you.

muscle relaxation

Many times we are holding tension in our bodies and don't really realize it is there. Relaxing those tight muscles can help you come back into balance. One way of doing this is to notice areas of tension in your body and first increase the tension in that area and then let go and release the tension. In doing so, people usually notice how much tension they have been holding and how good it feels to relax those muscles.

Where do you notice tension in your body? Is it in your shoulders? Your jaw? Wherever you experience tension, see if you can make that tension tighter. If it is in your shoulders, scrunch them up toward your ears. If it is in your jaw, clench your teeth. Hold that tension for a few seconds, and then let it go.

Repeat this a few times, and then really let yourself slide into that relaxation you are feeling after all that tension is released.

You might also notice where you feel tension in your body when you find it hard to feel compassion or acceptance for yourself. Beliefs, such as "I don't deserve compassion," can be held in the body—for instance, by our posture or the tension that is present in certain areas of the body.[63]

What do you notice when you change how you are sitting or standing or when you tighten and release those areas? Any shifts?

energy psychology techniques

There is a great deal of research demonstrating that energy psychology techniques calm the body. People report feeling calmer and these techniques have been shown to result in significant decreases in blood cortisol levels, a stress hormone.[64]

An example of an energy technique is focusing on troubling thoughts or feelings while gentle tapping or touching areas on the body associated with the energy systems in the body—for instance, the end points of the meridians. It is beyond the scope of this book for me to teach you how to use these techniques, and I have included a couple of links in the notes section of the book for those of you who would like to learn more about them.[65,66]

many ways to calm your system

There are many ways to relax your body enough to bring your thinking brain solidly back on board. These have simply been a few ideas. Because our social engagement system is so important in regulating our state, simple acts like looking into the eyes of someone who cares about you or hearing their voice may help you pop back into the middle.

Singing and humming are also great ways to shift the state of your nervous system. The long exhalation signals the body that all is well. Or you might listen to a guided meditation, do some yoga, pray, or watch or read something that triggers a good belly laugh.

Once you have shifted your system back into the middle, check to see if you can now feel self-compassion and acceptance. You may find that you were simply too stressed before and didn't have enough of your thinking brain on board for it to be possible to feel compassion.

If you continue to struggle with this, there are most likely unconscious beliefs or "wires" getting in the way. Working through the next sections may give you an idea of what is holding you back.

And don't forget to use your imagination as a way to mentally prepare yourself for the actual practice. Any or all of these approaches can be first practiced in the safety of your imagination.

Imagination works best when we are in a relaxed and calm state so be sure to use one of the ideas for calming your nervous system or listen to the connecting meditation before practicing these tools in your imagination.

When using your imagination, make sure to feel the rewards of self-compassion and acceptance. You are the director in the production you create with your imagination, so be sure to set it up so that you feel rewarded.

Cecilia used her imagination to feel more supported in her life. She did this by imagining herself having the support that she needed when she was young. Cecilia was excited to notice that in moments of stress, she felt this same support she had imagined for her younger self.

in a nutshell

- Self-acceptance is seeing yourself just as you are, and self-compassion is doing so with kindness, concern, and a willingness to help.

- Of all the steps in this model, this is the most important one.

- If you work on nothing else, work on loving self-acceptance and compassion.

- These skills are going to be essential in dealing with feelings that are bound to come up as you separate your worth from the approval of others.

- They will calm your nervous system and allow you to think and gain perspective.

- The wonderful thing about these skills is that *you can use them even if you don't feel you deserve them.* You can start with accepting and feeling compassion for the belief that you don't deserve acceptance or compassion.

- There are many ways to help you get started with feeling compassion for yourself, including metta meditation, feeling compassion for your younger self, or bringing in someone else to feel compassion for you.

- If none of these approaches helps or you feel stressed doing them, take a moment to bring your nervous system into balance.

- Maybe you were simply too far into the stress response to feel compassion.

- If you are struggling with this, keep working through the rest of the steps in the model. You may find there is an old assumption getting in the way or that there is some other need, like getting support.

- And, sometimes, you just need to keep practicing. Like any skill, the more you practice the easier it will become. Your brain will help you by creating new pathways, and the more you use them, the stronger they will become.

- So, keep practicing. You might be surprised.

- And don't forget about the power of mentally rehearsing feeling self-acceptance and compassion.

ideas for reflection

- What comes up for you when you think of accepting yourself right now, as you are?

- How about when you think of feeling self-compassion?

- How will you begin adding self-acceptance and compassion to your connections? What do you suppose will make it easier?

- How might you use imagery to mentally rehearse bringing these skills into your life?

chapter fourteen
"O": observing

In this step of the model, you will be adding observation to your connections. Observing your thoughts, feelings, and behaviors is going to be essential if you want to change the default wiring connecting your worth with approval. You can't change wiring without noticing it first. This step will help you do that.

Most times, the default wiring of this intimacy style is so automatic and feels so "right" that it is difficult for women to notice, especially in the beginning. Because of that, it is often easier to start by noticing feelings, and then work backward to the default wiring connecting approval with worth. To work backward in that way, you will need to get good at noticing and identifying your feelings.

why feelings?

Feelings are strong messengers from the body that something has shifted or is happening in the body or the brain. Feelings are the gateway to what is going on inside. As one of my client's so beautifully described it, "Feelings are like the red 'check engine light' on the dash of your car."

They are a signal to check in with what is happening inside of you and what is needed. Thoughts can be all over the place and can lead us on a wild goose chase when trying to figure out what is happening or what we need.

Have you ever tried to "figure out" what is going on inside and found one thought led to another until you'd uncovered a multitude of things that you were unhappy about, and then you felt worse than when you started?

Or have you ended up in an internal argument trying to convince yourself to think in a certain way? I bet you have tried to "talk" yourself out of needing the approval of others to feel good about yourself. I'm imagining if that would have worked, you wouldn't be reading this book.

The biggest problem with using thinking to try to change these circuits is that we can end up debating in our thinking brain and leaving the more primitive wires located in the emotional brain untouched.

Many of my clients knew, intellectually, that needing other's approval to feel good about themselves made no sense. And when they sensed disapproval, they were right back to not feeling okay about themselves.

Remember Margaret and her core belief that others needed to approve of her in order for her to be okay? When this wire wasn't lit up, she didn't believe that other people determined her worth and, in the moment, when the wiring of that core assumption was lit up, it was a different story. Can you think of an example of this in your own life? A time when intellectually you knew something wasn't true, and in the heat of the moment it *felt* true?

Now I'm not saying cognitive approaches are of no use or that we don't need to use our thinking to change, and my experience is that change is more lasting when you work with your feelings to bring to light old core wires that are triggering your reactions. Those wires aren't housed in our most recently developed thinking brain and in most cases, they aren't in your conscious awareness.

Most of them are developed in childhood when we operate primarily out of the emotional brain. Because of this, using emotions to access them is much more efficient.

Identifying feelings will help you identify these wires and give you the opportunity to bring new factual information into them. We will talk much more about this in the next chapter and to give you an idea of how feelings can lead to core assumptions, let me share an example.

using feelings to notice assumptions

The following is an example of how a client identified a core expectation by identifying her feelings. This client was in a group and was reluctant to participate. Here is my memory of that conversation.

Me: *What is your strongest feeling when you imagine speaking up in the group?*
Client: *It's fear.*
Me: *And can you put that in a sentence?*

Client: *I'm afraid that I will say the wrong thing.*

Me: *And if you say the wrong thing, what are you afraid will happen?*

Client: *They won't want me to be here.*

Me: *And what is scary about them not wanting you to be here?*

Client: *It means I'm not okay. That I'm not lovable. If I don't get things right, I'm not lovable.*

For this client, doing things right was wired with being lovable. In this moment, she felt the "truth" of that connection. She had just uncovered her core assumption about what was needed to be lovable, and this was the moment for her to bring new more reasonable information into this old circuit. We will talk about how she did that in the next chapter.

I hope that helps you understand how feelings can lead to discovering faulty wiring. We could have spent considerable time exploring all her negative experiences with speaking up and we may never have uncovered this core expectation that came up so quickly in her feelings.

To be clear, I'm not saying that every time you identify a feeling it will relate to a core belief or wire related to approval.

And checking in with your feelings will benefit you in other ways as you work on separating your worth from approval.

For all of us, observing our feelings helps us to better care for ourselves and to know what is important to us. For those with this intimacy style, who tend to notice their needs when way past their limits, connecting regularly with your feelings will give you the chance to catch feelings while they are small and before they grow so big that you feel the urge to disconnect and do damage to a relationship or your pride.

For now, I'm wondering how you are reacting to the notion of checking in with your feelings. Does it go something like this?

"I have no idea how I feel."

Most women with this intimacy style look at me with a "deer in the headlights look" when I ask what they are feeling. Part of the problem is that if you have this intimacy style, you most likely haven't been paying attention to yourself. Or, as Marshall Rosenberg, Ph.D., writes in his book *Nonviolent Communication: A Language of Life*

> *"For centuries, the image of the loving woman has been associated with sacrifice and the denial of one's own needs to take care of others. Because women are socialized to view the caretaking of others as their highest duty, they often learn to ignore their own needs."*[67]

So, if this feels like new territory, or you have no idea how you feel, that's understandable, and you certainly aren't alone.

The good news is that you are already skilled at noticing feelings in other people. This is the early training for anyone with an entangled intimacy style. You just need to use skills you already have with yourself.

let's build on your strengths

Since you excel at recognizing feelings in others, let's use that skill. Let's imagine that there is a part of you who holds your feelings. You might see her as a younger version of yourself or simply as a part of you that is the "feeler of your feelings." Many women find using a younger part of them or even the image of a child works best, as it is easy to imagine comforting a child.

And you can imagine her in any form that works for you. The important part is that you can feel caring and compassion for her and that you want to be her advocate.

I know some people have reactions to working with parts of themselves or doing "inner child work." If this is you, imagine you are checking in with your emotional brain to find out what is going on in there. Or you could imagine a friend in your situation and check in with how she might be feeling in your shoes.

And, if you want to skip all of that and go right to checking in with yourself just as you are, go for it! The important part is that you can notice what you are feeling, and you can do so with caring and compassion.

In connecting with the part of you who feels your feelings, you will be doing the same thing you do all day with other people. When you see someone, you get a sense of how they are feeling. For instance, if your roommate walks in, and she looks sad, I imagine it is pretty automatic to ask her what's up. You will be simply making an unconscious process conscious and turning it toward yourself. As you observe the feeler of your feelings, or your emotional brain, you are going to sense what she is feeling and put that into words.[68]

If you are using a younger version of yourself as the one who holds your feelings, it is important to remember that you are viewing this young self as *holding your current feelings*. You are imagining her as the one who feels sad when someone forgets your birthday or who feels tired when you do too much in a day.

At some point you may give your younger self the opportunity to express feelings from childhood, and that is not what we are doing here. In this exercise, you are simply picturing her as the one who feels your current feelings, right now in this moment.

the process

Picture the feeler of your feelings standing right out in front of you. Imagine what she looks like and see if you can feel love and compassion rising in your heart for her—this part of you who holds all your feelings.

Maybe you feel drawn to put your arm around her or you speak to her and let her know that you feel grateful that she carries your feelings for you. Maybe you let her know that you are there to listen and support her. After doing that, see if you can get a sense of what is going on inside her right now *in this moment*.

How is she doing physically? Is she rested or tired? Is she hungry, full, or had just enough?

Is she in pain or feeling sick? How about emotionally?

What is she feeling right now? Is she mad, sad, or afraid? Maybe feeling guilty or ashamed? Or lonely? Is she feeling happy or grateful? How about safe or secure?

Maybe loved or proud.

Help her to put her feelings into words. Start the sentence with "I feel" and then follow that with a feeling word and a *short* explanation. Using "I feel" is very important to the process. In doing so, you reinforce that these are feelings and not who you are.

So, it is not "I am angry;" it is, "I feel angry." Try to avoid long explanations that might bring up more feelings or make it hard to tell what is most important. And because feelings come from the more primitive part of our brain, they often sound "childlike." So, when you state your feelings, imagine the words a child would use. If you are using complicated or big words, you are most likely thinking rather than feeling. We want to find out what is happening in the body and the more primitive parts of the brain. These primitive words and sensations often connect to unreasonable assumptions that you will miss if you using complicated words coming from the thinking brain.

If I connect with my younger self to check on my feelings in this moment, she would say, *"I feel tired from working so hard outside today."* Recognizing this need doesn't connect me with faulty wiring and if I ignored being tired, I would likely slip into the stress response. As we talked about in chapter eleven—the mysterious middle, we are much more likely to trigger old fear wires when we move out of the middle and into stress.

If I ignored being tired, as I did with my shoveling, old wires related to my worth could easily be triggered. Much like mothers of young children learn to notice shifts in their children early—for instance when a child is a little cranky and before a temper tantrum—noticing your feelings early will save you from more intense reactions later.

If, when using your younger self to check in with your feelings, you end up feeling her feelings or you become overwhelmed by feelings from the past, try imagining a friend in your position instead of your younger self. Check in with how your friend would feel if she were in your shoes.

And, if you still find yourself overwhelmed with feelings, please reach out for support from your therapist. Sometimes beginning to care for yourself can stir up uncomfortable feelings.

check for the strongest feeling

Why is it important to check for your strongest feeling? Because your strongest feeling is going to give you the most specific information about what you need right now and will also lead you more directly to any old default wiring that is lighting up. We will talk about this in much more detail in the "offering" chapter. And I want to share an example that will hopefully spur your curiosity about your own unreasonable core assumptions.

This example illustrates how finding one's strongest feeling is helpful in self-care and how it can lead to the discovery of old faulty wiring. The most important take away from this example, is the importance of finding your strongest feeling. You will have other feelings and try to find the strongest one.

Remember Olivia, the athlete who was embarrassed about the size of her body? Olivia felt guilty about not going outside to exercise. She was caught in a vicious cycle. She felt guilty about not going out and then her guilt lowered both her mood and her motivation. This led to her staying inside and more guilt. Olivia initially believed guilt was her strongest feeling.

When I asked her to check inside and see if there were other feelings about not going out to move her body, a whole range of feelings came to the surface—among them was fear. When I asked her which was the strongest feeling, she was surprised that it was fear.

We engaged in a similar exploration to the one I shared with you earlier, taking each feeling statement a bit deeper, and this is what she uncovered.

> Olivia: *"If I go outside to walk or ride my bike, I feel afraid that people will see how fat I am."*
> Me: *"And what is scary about that?"*
> Olivia: *"I'm afraid I'll be judged."*
> Me: *"And if you are judged, what does that mean?"*
> Olivia: *"I shouldn't be out riding my bike when I am so fat."*

It took a few more steps, and Olivia realized that her weight determined whether she deserved to be out moving her body. The assumption was, *"I'm okay if I am thin."* And right below that was, *"I'm okay if others approve of me."*

If we would have stayed with her guilt about not moving her body, we might have spent a great deal of energy trying to come up with how she could let go of her guilt and get motivated to exercise.

We would have wasted time trying to solve the wrong problem. No matter how many strategies we came up with, if her brain was telling her that she wasn't okay until she was thin, the strategies would do no good. She wasn't going anywhere and risking not being "okay."

In the next chapter, we are going to talk about what to do once you have identified your strongest feeling or an unreasonable assumption. For now, practice identifying your strongest feeling and be curious about the possibility that an unreasonable assumption is driving that feeling.

If you can't tell which feeling is strongest or all your feelings feel strong, you have most likely tipped out of the middle and into the stress response. Noticing this is wonderful information. You now have a choice about what to do next rather than having your defaults take over and run the show.

When you notice that you have tipped out of balance this might be a great time to put your hand on your heart and feel some kindness or compassion for yourself or to practice one of the tools to relax your nervous system found on page 222.

you're going to need to practice

Like any skill, checking in on your feelings is not going to come naturally in the beginning. You will need a plan, and you will need to practice until it becomes a habit. Most women have found it easiest to add checking on their feelings to the connections they have already been doing.

If you have been having trouble getting those connections going, remember it is usually most helpful to pair them with something else in your day that you are already doing or to schedule them in your calendar.

And consider adding this step of noticing your feelings to any imagery or intention work you are doing in the morning. Imagine yourself staying connected with your internal life as you move through your day—noticing and naming feelings as they come up and feeling the reward of having done that.

As you get comfortable checking in and naming your feelings, try to do so often during your day. Simply take a moment to feel compassion, and then notice your strongest feeling. You might also begin to be curious about whether the feeling you identify is linked with an outdated assumption.

In the next chapter, we will talk about figuring out the need your strongest feeling is pointing you toward. For now, the goal is simply getting good at identifying your feelings.

in a nutshell

- In this step, you are going to begin observing or taking the "pulse of your inner life."

- In order to bring your needs back into the picture, you have to know what it is you need. Observing is the first step in doing that. It is also the first step in bringing new information into old faulty circuits.

- Feelings and body sensations are the most direct means of gathering information about what is happening inside and what you need.

- Most women struggle with knowing how they feel. If this is you, try imagining a part of you as the feeler of your feelings and checking in with her. This part might be your younger self.

- If you use your younger self, be sure to be check in with her about *your current feelings* rather than feelings from the past.

- And if you are having trouble observing rather than merging with the feelings your younger self is expressing, or feelings from childhood are coming up, try substituting a friend and imagine how she would feel if she were in your shoes.

- Be sure to check for your strongest feelings, as these give the most direct information about what you need.

- And be on the lookout for feelings associated with unreasonable outdated assumptions about yourself or your relationships with others.

- If you have difficulty identifying your strongest feeling or all your feelings feel strong, you have most likely tipped out of balance and into the stress response.

- If you have tipped out of balance, this might be a great time to put your hand on your heart and feel some kindness or compassion for yourself or to practice one of the tools to relax your nervous system found on page 222.

ideas for reflection

- What has been your experience with noticing or expressing your feelings? How might your previous experiences impact you as you check in on your feelings?

- What is it like to imagine a part of yourself as being the feeler of your feelings? Did checking in with her help you to identify your feelings? If not, how will you check in on your feelings?

- Were you able to feel compassion for your younger self or

the feeler of your feelings? How about a desire to be her advocate?

- What is it like for you to be putting your feelings into words?

- What patterns, if any, do you notice in checking in with your strongest feeling?

- What, if any, unreasonable assumptions did you uncover?

- Was there a time, during a connection, when you noticed that you were no longer in the middle? What steps did you take when you noticed this?

- When you notice your feelings, are they connected with any sensations in your body?

- Is a certain feeling connected with tension in a specific part of your body or a body posture? Noticing this connection will be another way of noticing your feelings in the future. For instance, what is your posture like when you feel sad? Where do you feel it in your body? How about fear and anger?

chapter fifteen
"O": offering

This step reminds you to give yourself what you need. There are several goals in giving yourself what you need, and because of that, this is a long chapter. To help with that, I have broken it up into four parts.

As you move through the chapter, keep your finger on the pulse of your inner life—staying connected with how responsive it is to continue reading or whether you need a break. You will get the most from this chapter by giving yourself time to reflect and to practice with the tools.

In the "Offering" step, we will be focusing on two goals.

1. Offering yourself good self-care. This step has four components.
   - Making sure you are in the middle.
   - Determining what you need.
   - Determining whether you can give yourself what you need

or whether you need to ask for support.

- And making sure that you follow through.

2. The second goal of the offering step is to bring new information into old, outdated assumptions linking your worth with approval.

chapter fifteen
part one

why self-care?

You might be wondering what self-care has to do with separating self-worth from approval. Without good self-care, you are going to find it difficult, if not impossible, to bring new information into the old default circuits linking your worth with approval. To bring in new information your thinking brain must be on board so that you can notice what is happening and decide what you want to happen next.

If you are too hungry, too tired, too overwhelmed, etc., your nervous system is going to detect a threat and mobilize the stress response rendering the thinking brain less effective. When this happens, it is much harder to notice and choose. So, giving yourself what you need to keep your body out of the stress response will be critical in rewiring old, outdated circuits.

Changing those old faulty circuits related to approval is also going to mean learning to deal effectively with feelings that are bound to come up when you face disapproval or rejection. Most times when women with this entangled intimacy style detect disapproval, the immediate reaction is to try harder to gain approval or they disconnect.

This is a trap. Finding relief through approval is an unending battle, and disconnecting usually comes at a cost. Learning to notice and deal with your feelings, even difficult feelings related to disapproval, is going to be necessary to change your old wires and it can free you from the trap of approval-seeking.

As I said at the beginning of the book, it is impossible to avoid judgment. You know this or you wouldn't be reading this book. Trying to be seen in a positive light to feel good about yourself just leads to a great deal of stress. There is always someone unhappy about something.

You will never have the chance to be yourself if you are waiting for everyone to give their permission. So, why not get good at dealing with fear and disappointment so that they don't derail you from being who you were meant to be in this world?

Learning to deal with feelings can set you free. People may disapprove, and you will know how to take care of yourself around the fear or guilt that might come up. And if you can use those feelings to change your wiring, their disapproval will no longer derail you. You might feel sad that they don't agree, and their disapproval will no longer define your worth.

There are so many reasons noticing what is going on inside and giving yourself what you need is important, and I want to mention one more before moving on to the nuts and bolts of figuring out what you need.

When you keep your finger on the pulse of your inner life, you can become aware of the chatter happening in the background of your mind. This will allow you to deal with it and in the process eliminate needless stress.

using feelings to bring yourself back to the present

When we are not consciously directing our attention, thoughts, or behaviors, the brain takes over and runs on our default wiring. As we talked about in an earlier chapter, this is necessary for us to accomplish all that we accomplish in a day.

The downside is that many of our defaults are worry wires about the past or the future. So, another big advantage of keeping your finger on the pulse of your inner life, is that you can notice and interrupt worry wires that may be triggering a stress response in your body when, in this moment, there is no reason for your body to be gearing up.

For instance, you might be relaxing on the couch in front of the TV and notice that you are feeling tense. By taking a moment to connect, you might notice that you are feeling afraid about giving a presentation at work.

You now have the chance to deal with this fear before it triggers a stress response—a response with lots of uncomfortable sensations in your body not the least bit conducive to relaxing on the couch.

Having your finger on your pulse and dealing with feelings when they are small can help you avoid tipping into the desperate state where it will feel like your life is hanging in balance, when in fact you are at home safe on your couch.

And I'm imagining that for some of you reading the title of this section, you wondered, "What time relaxing on the couch watching television?"

one layer of stress is enough, isn't it?

I recognize that most women lead very stressful lives with lots of balls in the air and few moments truly to themselves. You may not even remember a time when you were able to sit and relax on the couch or watch a show on television.

And what many of us do is add another layer of stress to the stress that is already there. While trying to get kids to school on time, we are worrying about an interaction we had at work or beating ourselves up for carrying so much extra weight, or for not being active at our child's school, our church, or with a volunteer organization, etc.

Remember, the body doesn't differentiate between what we are imagining and what's actually happening, so when you are worrying about your weight or an interaction at work, your body will interpret those worries as current threats. Adding those stressors to the stress that is already there in getting kids to school on time may be enough to trigger a full-blown stress response.

Being tipped or in a full-blown stress response is problematic in and of itself. It's uncomfortable; it interferes with being productive, and we often do some type of damage either to ourselves or to others when we are tipped. It will also work against you as you try to disconnect the link between your worth and approval.

When you are tipped into the stress response, the thinking on this faulty wiring is going to *feel* factual. Disapproval will feel devastating, and you will believe that it means something about your worth.

A look or a comment that might go unnoticed in balance will be interpreted as being personal when you are tipped.

And if approval is wired with safety, you are going to feel driven to seek approval. This isn't a defect in you, it is the functioning of the emotional brain using past experience to predict how to keep you safe.

Unfortunately, each time we go down the path of approval seeking we strengthen that wiring, making it even more likely to fire in the future during stress.

Because of this, recognizing when you are tipped is going to be essential if you want to change these wires. So, let's spend a few minutes reviewing the differences between being in the middle and being tipped.

the world through "tipped eyes"

We talked about this before and being able to recognize your state—meaning whether you are tipped or in emotional balance, is so critical to both your self-care as well as in your work on changing old wires related to approval, that I want to spend a bit more time on it.

How we see the world and what we believe is very different when we are tipped out of balance than it is when we are in the middle and in emotional balance. This has to do with the part of the brain which is dominant during each of these states.

Take a moment and compare your reactions when you are tipped as compared to when you are feeling in balance. It's easier to take things in stride or to put things into perspective when you're calm, isn't it?

When I drive home from town on a day when I am in emotional balance, I am likely to notice the beauty of the mountains. I'm also less bothered by the traffic.

In contrast, on a day when I'm tipped, the view might as well not be there, and the stop lights seem to know that I am coming. How about you? What do you notice when you are in emotional balance as compared to times when you are tipped?

How about when a friend doesn't call you? How might your reactions differ depending on whether you are in balance or tipped? In a calm state, if a friend doesn't call, I imagine you might feel empathy for all she has on her plate or wonder if she is okay.

The ability to see beauty, to have empathy, as well as to think about what it is like to be in someone else's shoes are all abilities of the thinking brain.

In the middle, with a fully functioning thinking brain, we can put things in perspective, and we are less likely to take things personally—like the changing of the stop lights.

When we are tipped and the emotional brain is running the show, we are highly ego-centric—things are about us and personal. "It's just my luck that I would hit every red light!"

Think about how you might react to a friend not calling when your kids haven't listened to a single thing you've said, or you are dead tired from trying to meet a million deadlines at work *and* have some type of social life. Your reaction would probably be different, wouldn't it?

When something like this happens when we are tipped, we are likely to either believe the other person is wrong, "She's not a very good friend not to keep in touch." Or that we're wrong, "I wonder what I did to upset her?"

This is the either/or concrete thinking that occurs when the emotional brain is dominant when we are tipped. Either way, it is personal.

The ability to take a wide-lens perspective or to have empathy for others goes out the window. The emotional brain is all about helping us see potential danger so that we can stay safe.

And it is better to be safe than sorry—a good strategy for predators and not that great of a strategy when it comes to relationships. Expecting the worst in relationships is bound to cause strain.

When the primitive emotional brain is running the show when we are tipped, we're likely to draw false conclusions that damage both our own sense of self, as well as our relationships. So, before you make any decisions about what you need, it is crucial to be sure that you are in the middle.

are you in the middle?

Take a moment and go back and review the differences you just came up with for when you are tipped as compared to when you are in balance. You might also go back and look at your snapshot for being tipped that you worked on in chapter 10.

What is your thinking like when you are tipped? What emotions tend to come up? Are there certain behaviors that are indicators that you have tipped—maybe the urge to tell people off or to surf the cupboards or the fridge?

Most women find their thinking, emotions, and behaviors while tipped to be fairly predictable. For instance, one of my clients realized that when tipped, she often questioned the purpose of her life, felt exhausted, and often withdrew.

Once she realized that these thoughts and feelings were there each time she was tipped, they became like an indicator light for her that she was tipped.

Another client's thoughts centered around being alone in the world. She felt jealous of women with spouses and would move into panic if she stayed tipped for any length of time.

Whenever she heard herself saying or thinking, "I'm all alone," she knew that she was tipped. Other women knew they were tipped when their thinking started spinning or when all their emotions felt intense.

It is important to know what happens for you when you are tipped so that you will recognize it. Knowing your state is also essential in deciding what you need.

Before the client that I mentioned a moment ago realized that believing her life lacked purpose was a faulty wire that lit up when she was tipped, each time she was tipped she felt an intense need to figure out her life purpose.

This was a waste of time, as when she was in balance, her life felt purposeful. Unfortunately, every time she went down that bunny trail related to lacking a life purpose, it also strengthened that circuit making it stronger and more likely to fire up again when she felt stressed.

I hope these examples have helped you to understand how crucial it is to be in emotional balance or in the middle when deciding what you need.

When you are tipped, there is a strong drive for immediate relief with no regard for the consequences. *The only need we have when tipped is to get back in balance.* Let me say that again as this is really important. The only thing you need to focus on when you are tipped is getting yourself back into the middle and balance.

Some questions to ask yourself to determine whether you are in the middle and in emotional balance include,

- Can I think about the consequences of my actions—what I might regret?
- Can I see more than one side to the situation I'm in?
- Can I put this incident in perspective and see it as one aspect of the larger picture of my life or my relationship?
- Can I *feel* compassion for the people involved, including myself?
- Can I put myself in their shoes and *feel* empathy or understanding for their position?

If you notice yourself using words like "always" and "never," you have slipped out of the middle. Rarely in life are things absolute. This concrete, absolute perspective is the perception of the emotional brain—most likely gearing us up to protect ourselves.

Since most women with this intimacy style connect with their needs when they are past their limits or have had it, these questions will also help you to be sure to check that you haven't tipped and swung over to disconnecting where you are only focused on your needs. Making decisions while disconnected feels good in the moment and usually isn't worth it, unless of course you are in danger and need to think only of yourself.

If you find that you have disconnected or tipped into a stress response, do your best not to judge yourself, as in fact, you have just accomplished a difficult feat.

noticing takes skill

If you noticed that you have tipped or swung over to disconnecting, this is a huge accomplishment. It takes practice and skill to notice when we are tipped.

So, if you have noticed this swing or slip, your practice connecting with yourself is paying off. Please take a moment to underline the work you have done and feel the reward.

Now you can make a choice to care for yourself rather than letting your default wiring lead you right back into your old patterns.

It's important to realize that in the moment it may not *feel* so great to apply the brakes before speaking or acting. And being able to stop and choose a different path despite the pull to act, is a moment for celebration.

Noticing that you have tipped and interrupting your defaults is the way you begin to lay down new pathways in your brain. You can't change what you haven't noticed or interrupted.

If you find you aren't in balance, take a moment to use one of the practices to relax your nervous system found on page 222.

Or try writing out all the components of your experience. Write your feelings, thoughts, behaviors, and body sensations as you did in the ideas for reflection section of chapter thirteen—the mysterious middle.

Doing this will help you reflect on the situation and will often help you pop back into the middle. It may also help you notice any unreasonable assumptions that may have pulled you out of balance. Once you are back in the middle, you can more securely check in with your needs.

If you aren't yet noticing when you have tipped or swung over to disconnecting until after the damage is done, please don't be hard on yourself. It is hard to interrupt the pull to action from the emotional brain. And the good news is you noticed.

And from my own experience, even noticing right afterward may be difficult in the beginning. It is far easier to work with small blips than a full-blown stress response.

start with drills, not a tournament

Most times when I introduce these skills to clients, I hear something like, *"Okay, the next time I feel stressed, I'll try this."* When I hear that, I encourage my clients, and I want to encourage you, not to wait until you are stressed to work on these skills.

Waiting until you are tipped or stressed to work on the skills in this book is like trying to learn tennis by signing up for a tennis tournament.

Just as you might decide tennis is not for you by holding a racket for the first time in a tennis tournament, you are very likely to decide that these skills are impossible or not for you if you wait until you are stressed to try them.

With enough practice you will be able to use these skills in the heat of the moment, and just like with tennis, you will need a lot of practice before you find a "tournament" rewarding. Until then, working on the small wobbles will be more rewarding and effective.

catching the small wobbles

I often share with clients that we are like wobble dolls—those dolls with the rounded bottoms. Without our awareness, the emotional brain constantly surveys the environment for danger both from the outside—like from a predator or someone's disapproval—and from inside—from our thoughts or the condition of the body such as exhaustion or being too hungry. Because of this, we tend to frequently wobble or tip out of balance.

Keeping your finger on the pulse of your inner life, catching small changes that require your attention, and giving yourself what you need will give you the best chance of preventing small wobbles from turning into a full-blown stress response, where you will be vulnerable to old assumptions as well as concrete and catastrophic thinking.

think temper tantrum

It has often helped my clients to think of a full-blown stress response or a tip into the desperate state as the adult version of a temper tantrum. As adults, we just have more options besides the flailing and screaming a two-year-old does during a temper tantrum. If you think of a child having a temper tantrum, what are you likely to do?

You're going to try to stay calm, wait for it to pass, and work on containment—making sure that they don't hurt themselves or others, right?

I was sharing this idea with a client the other day, and a memory came up of staying with a friend of mine and her little boys. It was the night before I was to leave and the youngest, who was sad about me leaving, suddenly yelled out, *"I hate you, Deb."*

I imagine he was feeling powerless. I was leaving, and there was nothing he could do about it. He was feeling desperate, and his desperation turned to anger. It hurt to hear those words, and I knew they weren't true.

Hearing this example really helped my client realize that what we think and feel when we are tipped isn't factual. It is coming from the primitive emotional regions of our brain and is a desperate attempt to get what we *think we need* in that moment.

It is important to realize this is just your body in stress, that it will pass, *even though it doesn't feel like it will*. Remember a temper tantrum. In the moment, it can feel like it will be never-ending, and it ends. And remember the words of the little boy who yelled that he hated me. This is not the time to make decisions or to believe your thinking.

I bring this up because often clients have become discouraged along the way while working on these skills because they had been believing their thinking when they were tipped. Just like my friend's son who didn't actually hate me, your thoughts while tipped aren't factual. These are feelings coming from the primitive brain. Feelings are not the same thing as facts.

Thinking about tipping in this way can also help you to be kinder to yourself when you do notice that you are tipped. Just like that child flailing their arms and legs, you too have reached a limit. You may say and do things you regret.

it happens to the best of us

Remember earlier in the book when I described feeling confused when matching what my clients wrote on their paperwork with the women who were sitting with me. This was because, at least initially, I wasn't seeing them in a tipped state. These calm women acted very differently when they were tipped, just as I act and think very differently when I'm tipped.

While working with Laurel Mellin, Ph.D., I once heard her say that we are more like each other in a tipped state than we are like ourselves in balance.[69] The reason for this is that in a tipped state, each of our emotional brains is focused on the same thing, our own survival. And without the resources of the thinking brain, we each lack awareness of the impact of our choices on our own lives, as well as on the lives of others.

You're going to tip. What we want to get good at is noticing the tip early, before we are in the desperate state—or even better, when we first notice the "check engine" light coming on. We want to get good at preventing a tip if we can and bouncing back when we do tip. Meeting your needs is going to help you do that.

Before we move on to talking about how to determine what you need, let's stop here so that you can spend some time reviewing what you have read so far and be sure you have a pretty good idea of the signs that you are tipped so you can recognize when it happens.

in a nutshell

- In the offering step of the model, there are two goals: first, bringing new information into old automatic default wiring linking your worth with approval, and second, offering yourself the care that you need to maintain emotional balance.

- Without good self-care, you are going to find it difficult, if not impossible, to bring new information into the old default circuits linking your worth with approval.

- When we ignore our needs, we are likely to tip out of emotional balance limiting our ability to think and choose and leaving us more vulnerable to concrete and catastrophic thinking.

- Learning to meet your needs will help you deal more effectively with your feelings when you experience disapproval.

- Another advantage of keeping your finger on the pulse of your inner life is that you can notice when internal chatter may add another layer of stress to your already stressful life.

- Besides being uncomfortable, being tipped interferes with being productive, and we often do some type of damage either to ourselves or to others while tipped.

- How we see the world and what we believe is very different when we are tipped out of balance than it is when we are in the middle and in emotional balance.

- When we are in the middle or in balance, we can see beauty, feel connected with others, feel empathy and compassion, and think about all aspects of a situation and the consequences of our actions.

- None of these abilities are possible when we have tipped. While tipped our thinking is very concrete. We are likely to use words like always and never, and we tend to see others as being all wrong or ourselves as being all wrong.

- It is important to develop a snapshot of what you "look like" when you are tipped so you can begin to recognize when you are in the middle and when you are tipped.

- Recognizing when you are tipped is going to be essential if you want to change old faulty wires.

- Noticing that you have tipped is a moment for celebration! It takes skill to notice when we are tipped, so be sure to underline your accomplishment.

- Start your practice of these skills with the "small wobbles" rather than when you are tipped or in the desperate state. Start with drills and not a "tournament."

- Remember that we all tip. One way of thinking of a tip into the desperate state is to think of it as the adult version of a temper tantrum. You have simply gone past your limits or resources. Remember that it will pass and do your best not to believe your thinking during these times.

ideas for reflection

- What changes in your self-care might make it easier to stay in the middle or in balance?

- Think of some examples where you kept your finger on the pulse of your inner life and gave yourself what you needed. How about times when you ignored your inner life or checked in with your feelings and didn't follow through? What differences do you notice?

- Can you think of an example of a time when a worry came up during a time when you were relaxing? How might the experience be different if you noticed the worry and gave yourself what you needed versus ignoring it?

- Pick an example from your life and describe how it would be different when tipped as compared to when you are in balance.

- Think of an example of how deciding what you need while tipped might do damage. I'll start you off. Remember when I was doing all of that shoveling and I said that if there had been someone here in the house, I bet I would have come in and let them have it? Needing to let someone have it may have seemed reasonable while tipped and if I had followed through, I would have regretted it. What kinds of things might you say or do while tipped that you might regret or which might cause damage?

- Has there been a time when you noticed you were tipped? Please describe and be sure to underline all the work you have done to get to the place where you can notice being tipped!

Yahoo!

chapter fifteen
part two

what do you need?

Years ago, I was asked by a nurse practitioner to be a guest speaker in a course on emotional eating she was offering in the community. I was talking about the idea of feelings and needs, and the nurse practitioner said,

"Well, the idea of checking in with feelings makes sense, and you lost me with figuring out what I would need."

She certainly hasn't been the only one. Figuring out what is needed tends to stump most women in the beginning. The reason for this is that there is a tendency to overcomplicate the answer. Instead of coming up with the need for the moment, most tend to analyze the situation or try to solve it for the future.

Let me use my feeling of being tired to help explain what I mean. When I checked in, my strongest feeling was physically tired. So, what do I need?

If you had a physically exhausted child, the answer to the question of what the child needs would be simple, right? They need to rest or sleep. You're going to sit your child down in a comfy chair with a book or settle them in for a nap.

What I don't imagine you would do is have a lengthy discussion with them about all the reasons they feel tired and what they might do differently the next time.

That might be something to think about in the future. And, having that discussion when your child is exhausted is probably going to push them over the edge, making it worse for both of you.

I'm imagining this makes total sense thinking about a child and at the same time, when it comes to determining what you need, you might find yourself going down the "lengthy discussion" path.

The reason most people get stumped with figuring out what they need is that instead of solving the problem of the moment, they try to solve the problem for the rest of their life.

So, when you are thinking of what you need, the question is, *"What do I need right now?"* Not for the rest of your life or even tomorrow—simply right now in this moment in time. And the answer is specific to the feeling.

For me, I am not sleepy tired; I probably wouldn't sleep if I went to bed, and a nice warm bath sounds like just the right fit for my body that is tired from the physical work of shoveling snow. You might be thinking, *"Well, that was an easy one."* Or *"I know how to deal with my physical needs, it's my emotions that throw me."*

I purposely chose a physical need to start with, as for most people the answer tends to come up more quickly and be clearer. The answer lies in what would bring relief. The same is true for emotional needs. And the answer lies in what would bring relief in this moment in time.

emotional needs

When I ask my clients what they might need when the strongest feeling is an emotion, most times I hear *"I don't know what the need is. What could I do about that?"* Let's start with sadness, as most often women are confused by what they might need when it comes to sadness. I ask them to put it into a sentence. "I feel sad that..." and then to think about what they might need.

After they have done that, if they are still stumped, I ask them to imagine a child in front of them feeling sad and saying those words. Usually, the answer becomes obvious. I hear things like, *"I'd give them a hug"* or *"I'd tell them I understand."* Or I would say, *"Of course."* or *"I'm right here with you."*

What would feel good to you when you're feeling sad? When you figure out the care that you need, try to be as specific as you can so you know exactly what you are going to offer yourself or ask for from someone else.

a simple question

A simple way of checking to see if what you have decided you need is going to be helpful is to imagine the part of you who holds your feelings. Will what you are offering calm her or ramp her up? Will she feel seen and cared for?

Or if you are checking in on your emotional brain rather than the feeler of your feelings, you could ask yourself will what I am about to offer calm or rev up my emotional brain?

Let's say my strongest feeling is fear. And this is what I heard from my feeling part, *"I feel afraid that they won't like me anymore if I don't go to the party."*

And what if my response is, *"Don't worry about what they think."* Will that response help the scared part of me to feel calmer and more secure? I doubt it. I'm imagining my feeling part might need to hear something like,

> *"I hear how scary this is for you. I really don't believe that your friends will stop liking you if you don't go. They might be disappointed, and if they are your friends they will understand. How about let's not worry about their reactions until we know how they react. If we need to, we will figure out what to do. No matter what, I will be here with you to help you."*

Take a moment and think of the words that would calm your scared part feeling that fear. What would she need to hear? The words your scared part needs to hear may be different from mine. This is an opportunity to tap into *your* wisdom. Remember my example of reaching out to my friend and not getting the response I hoped for? I knew best what I needed to hear, and so do you.

As you move forward, remember to ask yourself as you observe and offer, "Am I stressing or calming the part of me who feels my feelings—or my emotional brain?" This one sentence alone can be a quick and easy tool to use as you move through your day.

If you are having trouble determining your strongest feeling and what you need, it may be that you have tipped out of balance. It is very difficult to observe and be discerning when the thinking brain is off-line.

If you realize that you are tipped, no matter how much you want to slip away or let the other person have it, see if you can get yourself back into the middle before deciding how to proceed.

And if you can't seem to get to the middle, there is most likely an old unreasonable assumption that is preventing you from coming back into balance.

We will talk about how to work with these old assumptions in the next section. For now, take some time to review and think about what you have just read.

in a nutshell

- Most women struggle with figuring out what they need after they have identified how they feel.

- The problem tends to be that instead of focusing on what is needed right now in this moment to get relief, most try to solve the problem for their lifetime.

- The answer is what brings relief right now whether the feeling is a physical one, like being too tired, or an emotion like sadness.

- If you struggle with identifying the need for feelings, imagine a young child in front of you expressing the feeling. Most times, the answer comes up pretty quickly.

- This is a chance to tap into your own wisdom. What you need may be very different from what anyone else needs, and that is okay. Your job is to match what you offer with the need or feeling.

- As you move forward identifying your feelings and needs, be sure to check in with the feeler of your feelings or your emotional brain to be sure that what you have offered has been calming.

- If you are struggling to figure out what you need, it may be that you have tipped out of balance. Remember, we can't observe when the thinking brain is off-line.

- If you are having trouble getting yourself back into balance, there may be an old assumption that is fueling your thoughts and feelings. We will talk more about that in the next section.

ideas for reflection

- What feelings come up when you think about meeting your own needs? Do you feel lost? Is any resentment coming up? If so, describe.

- Which feelings are the most difficult for you to figure out what you need? What is it like if you imagine a child in front of you expressing those feelings? Does that make it easier? If you are still stuck, what do you imagine you might say to a friend feeling that feeling?

- If you are checking in on your feelings by imagining a part of you who feels your feelings, do you have a clear image of that part? How old is she? What is she wearing? How long is her hair? Try to really "see" her. If you can't visualize her, no worries. What is your sense of what she is like?

- After you offered yourself what you needed, how did the

feeler of your feelings respond? Did what you offered calm her? If not, what might?

- If you are unable to answer the question of what you need, you have most likely slipped out of the middle. What might help you come back into balance? No worries if you are stuck, we will explore how old expectations can keep us fired up in the next section.

chapter fifteen
part three

old unconscious assumptions

At the end of the last section, I mentioned that if you are tipped and having trouble getting yourself back into balance, an old assumption may be keeping you stuck.

These assumptions are tricky as they are most often not in our conscious awareness. When they light up, what we usually notice is the result—intense feelings or that we are tipped and can't seem to get back in balance.

Let's spend some time talking about how these assumptions develop and how to bring new information into them.

where they come from

These unconscious beliefs or assumptions are most often formed when we are young at a time when all of us, as children, are drawing conclusions about ourselves, relationships, and the world. Because we are doing so with an immature brain, we lack the ability to understand the complexities of life and relationships and as a result, many if not most, of these beliefs are not reasonable or factual.

These beliefs are stored as implicit memories or memories that are outside of our conscious awareness. Without our awareness, these beliefs become the foundation for how we see the world, ourselves, and others. We rarely realize that these beliefs are guiding our thinking as well as our behaviors.

When these wires are lit up, we experience the thoughts, feelings and body sensations associated with the wire and because we don't realize an old wire has been triggered, we most often attribute our reactions to the current situation rather than to old, outdated wiring. We are unaware that we are viewing the present through the lens of old unreasonable assumptions most often formed in childhood.

Let's look at an example of how one of these wires might develop and the impact it may have in adulthood.

Imagine that in childhood, I hear over and over that I must be quiet. Maybe my mother is noise sensitive, and when I am noisy, she becomes irritable. When I am quiet, she is much calmer and as a result more able to be attentive and loving toward me.

Because when I am quiet I feel more loved, my immature brain will likely connect being quiet with being loved. This relationship will be wired sturdily in my brain because love is connected with survival and keeping us safe is a priority for the brain.

This wire is likely to light up in relationships or social situations, or possibly even when I need to mow the lawn—all in an effort to keep me quiet and therefore safe.

In these situations, I won't understand why I am afraid or anxious, and I might decide that I lack confidence or have social anxiety. I might even decide that it's just easier to be alone.

Or maybe I decide to tackle my anxiety and take a class designed to increase my confidence and help me feel less anxious in social situations.

To my dismay and frustration, the more confident I become

about speaking up the more anxiety I feel. I am totally unaware of the connection that has been formed in my brain between staying quiet and being loved—and as a result, don't understand why I am more anxious the more confident I become about speaking up.

As this example illustrates, a big part of the problem with these old assumptions is that they are operating outside of our conscious awareness. Another problem is that they are isolated from the rest of our brain.

isolated wiring

I once read an analogy, written by a neuroscientist, comparing these old wires to soldiers left on an island during a war. I love this analogy and have used it many times with clients since reading it. Unfortunately, I can't remember the original source. If you are reading this and know the source, please let me know so I can credit the author.

While the soldiers are on the island, the war ends. The soldiers are left there on the island unaware that the war is over. So, they continue to watch for danger and are ready to fight.

This is such a great way of picturing our old wires—they are isolated and don't have any current accurate information.

On the island, you believe the war is still going on. In the case of the wire, when it is lit up and you are "on" that wire, you believe whatever beliefs and feelings are encoded on the wire.

If a wire was formed in your early childhood, when that wire lights up, your thinking and reasoning will be like that of a child, and your emotions will reflect the experiences of childhood.

There might be fear or a feeling of powerlessness because when we are young, we have very little power—we can't change the rules or up and leave if we don't like how things are going.

The soldiers need to know that the war is over so that they can relax, and the wires isolated in your emotional brain need new, more accurate information—for instance, that you are no longer a powerless child without the ability to choose. Or in the example I just shared, that I don't need to be quiet to be loved.

These wires also need connections with the rest of the brain so that when a wire lights up, so does the ability to reflect on what you are feeling. We need to bring these wires into our conscious awareness, bring in new more current information, and connect them with other parts of the brain. Let's talk about how you might go about doing that.

bringing new information into old wires

The first step in working with these wires is realizing they are there or identifying them. As I just mentioned when they fire up, you will feel the effects of the wire—you might be overwhelmed with thoughts and feelings, or you might feel the urge to act in some way. If you have this intimacy style you will likely be pulled to either appease or disconnect.

What you most likely won't be aware of is the underlying assumption or belief that is driving all of that intensity. Paying attention to your feelings can help you identify the core assumption driving those feelings. Once you have identified a core assumption, you now have the opportunity to go to the root of your upset rather than being caught up trying to remedy the ramifications of the wire in your life.

a moment of opportunity

When you have uncovered an old unreasonable belief or assumption it may not feel like it at the time, and this is a moment of opportunity. Here's what I mean by that.

To change old beliefs, we have to notice them when they are fired up or "hot." So, when you have stayed with your feelings until you uncovered the assumption that is fueling them, this is the moment when you have the chance to create change in that wire. That is what I mean by it being a moment of opportunity.

Let me back up for a moment. Our knowledge of the brain is constantly changing with advancements in technology. We once believed that once implicit memories and the beliefs contained within them were formed or "consolidated" they were there to stay. That there was no way for us to change them.

At the time of the writing of this book, thinking has shifted, and we now believe that these implicit memories or beliefs can change, or be reconsolidated, under certain conditions. Reconsolidation means that these wires are put back together in a new way—that the wire is no longer the same as it was before, and the assumptions of the wire have been changed in some way.

There seem to be three conditions that allow reconsolidation of these wires that are outside of our awareness.[70,71]

necessary conditions for change

The first required condition is that the wire of the old assumption needs to be lit up or "hot." This means we feel it—often in the body. It feels true. Clients have often shared that it, *feels true right down to my core.*

For instance, when Margaret said aloud her faulty expectation related to approval, she felt swamped by fear. The wire was definitely "hot."

The second condition is that we are in enough emotional balance to be able to observe our experience and realize that an old wire has been triggered. We have at least "one foot" off the wire so that we can observe it and think about it.

When Margaret was on the wire, she felt terrified of doing anything that would displease her husband. Her belief was, *"To be 'okay' and a good person, I need to keep people happy. If I don't, I won't be loved, and I will be alone."*

This was her reality most of the time because, remember, these old beliefs become the lens through which we view the world.

Over time Margaret gradually felt less and less fear as she said, or thought about, this belief and at some point, she was able to see that the words and feelings triggering her fear represented an old belief rather than the "facts." She was able to view the belief for what it was—an old assumption.

In doing that, she had just met the second condition necessary for reconsolidation of the wire. She was in enough emotional balance to notice the assumption and think about whether it was reasonable.

This is what I meant earlier when I mentioned that when you become aware of an unreasonable assumption it is a moment of opportunity. At this point, you now have the chance to change the nature of the wire by bringing in new information that contradicts or is a "mismatch" to the existing information on the wire.

Even though I described it as "a moment" of opportunity, you actually have quite a bit more time than a moment, as the wire stays amenable to change for five to six hours after it lights up. So, you have some time to regain balance and add new factual information.

When Margaret was able to notice that she was triggered by her old wire and feel the truth of the fact that her husband could be upset with her and still love her, she was bringing new contradictory information into the old faulty assumption.

When the old wire was triggered or hot, she was able to notice and feel the truth of information that contradicted or discredited the original assumption.

Since this process is going to be so important, let's take a moment and talk a bit more about how you might bring contradictory information to an old wire.

what are the facts?

Once you follow your feelings to the core assumption fueling those feelings and you are in enough balance to be aware that it is an assumption, you now have an opportunity to bring new, current *factual information* into that wire.

I put the word "factual" in italics, as it is important that the information you bring in is factual rather than just what *feels* true. In deciding what the truth is that you want to bring into the new wire, be sure you are still in the middle and haven't disconnected.

Here's an example of what I mean by that. Let's say a woman has the old faulty assumption that *"to be okay and loved I need to be thin."* And after discovering it, she says, *"The fact is I don't care what anyone thinks, my body is my body!"*

This statement does bring in contradictory information to the original belief of, "I need to be thin to be loved," and it is true that her body is her body, and can you detect the element of disconnection in her statement—the "I don't care what anyone thinks"?

When we have disconnected, the idea that we don't care what others think can feel *so* true. It can *feel* like the truth of what needs to come into the wire. And because most women are filled with fear, guilt, and even shame after disconnecting, they most often swing right back over to appeasing and no longer believe what they believed while disconnecting.

As a result, even though the information "felt" true in that moment of disconnection and it did contradict the information on the original wire, it doesn't "stick."

In other cases, instead of disconnecting, women end up right back on the original wire. For instance, a woman might say something like, *"But, I do believe that I won't be lovable until I'm thin."*

If you find yourself in this situation, try asking yourself, *"What would you think if your daughter said those words?"* or, if you don't have a daughter, *"What would you think if those were the words of a good friend?"*

Would you say, *"Yep, you are right. I could only love you if you are thin"?*

Usually thinking about this pops clients right back into balance as they realize they would never believe that their daughter or good friend needed to be thin to be loved.

Did you notice that I said, "thinking about this"? These questions require you to think, which engages the thinking brain and helps you come back into balance.

When we are in balance, there is a much better chance of recognizing that what we are saying, or an old belief isn't factual.

And sometimes women really struggle with what to do if they don't believe what they have come up with to contradict the wire.

To help with that, let's go back to the example of being bitten by a dog. Sometimes, it's just easier to understand something by thinking of an entirely different situation.

working with a fear of dogs

Because being bitten was painful and frightening, my brain will have recorded that memory and will be on the lookout for dogs to help me be prepared and stay safe.

And because the emotional brain works on the premise of better safe than sorry, the assumption will be that all dogs are dangerous. So, any time I encounter a dog, I will see that dog as dangerous and feel fear. This belief will become the lens through which I see dogs.

Unless I want to avoid all dogs, I am going to need to bring new, contradictory information into the belief that all dogs are dangerous. For instance, if I know for a fact that not all dogs bite and I believe it when say it, I could notice the fear and feel the truth of the fact that not all dogs bite. So, while the wire is hot, I'm in enough balance to notice it, and I believe the information I am saying to dispute the fear.

what if I don't believe the new information?

And if I say that all dogs don't bite and don't believe it, the wire is going to stay the same, because the fear is still there.

I will need to do some work to get to the place where I can say with confidence and believe that not all dogs bite. For instance, I might need to observe dogs from a distance or be around friends who have friendly dogs.

Or I might need to gain some new knowledge about dogs by researching signs of an aggressive dog or by learning the safest ways to approach a strange dog. I may still have the fear response in seeing a new dog, and it will be tempered by the connection with this knowledge in my thinking brain.

As I gain more knowledge and positive experiences with dogs, the fear portion of this wiring will decrease and be replaced by other thoughts, experiences, and emotions, perhaps the joy of petting or playing with a happy dog.

There may always be some fear, which is not a bad thing, as maintaining some healthy fear of unfamiliar animals keeps us safe.

Like dealing with wires related to a fear of dogs, where you are going to start with bringing new information into old faulty assumptions about approval will depend on the degree of fear that comes up when you think about changing them.

can you feel it?

A good way to figure out where the starting place is for you in bringing in new, contradictory, information into an old wire is by, you guessed it, checking in with your feelings.

To help explain what I mean, let's go back to the dog bite. If I was terrified during that experience, it will most likely not work to tell myself, "Don't be afraid—not all dogs bite." I'm still going to be feeling the fear of being bitten and my brain is going to pay more attention to the fear than my words.

I can share this with certainty because of my own experience of being attacked by a pack of stray dogs when I was in my late 20s. The animal control officer who sat with me afterward told me not to show fear when facing wild dogs. That man may as well have been speaking a foreign language.

My brain was filled with fear remembering those dogs coming at me and being bitten. Luckily for me, the dogs weren't intent on harming me, and only one dog got in a good bite before they moved on. And I was terrified of encountering them again.

how I worked with this fear wire

It took many encounters with other dogs and talking with many dog trainers before I could start believing the new information that needed to come into the wire.

Once I believed it, I had to notice the fear when it was there and at the same time bring in knowledge and perspective from my thinking brain that I was able to believe and feel the truth of—for instance, that encountering a pack of wild dogs was an isolated incident and not one that I could expect to happen every day and with every group of dogs.

When I felt the fear, I repeatedly reminded myself that not all dogs are dangerous and that I had walked that road hundreds of times and not seen those dogs. I also reminded myself that I had survived. I felt secure when I said that to myself, which motivated me to keep working on it.

As a result, I changed my unreasonable assumption from "all dogs are dangerous and will attack" to a more reasonable fact-based assumption that "not all dogs are dangerous, and I can trust myself to do the best that I can if I encounter a dog or dogs that are dangerous." I now also set a positive intention of arriving home safely and feel the reward of having done so before setting out in areas with known predators.

start where you are

Like my process of dealing with my fear of being bitten by a dog, you will need to start where you are in working with the wires connecting your worth with approval. If you can tell yourself that the assumption you discovered isn't factual and you can feel the truth of what you are saying and feel some reward in stating the new belief, that's great. You are ready to bring new information into the old wire. If instead it brings up more fear, you are going to need to back up.

Let me share an example of what I mean by that. Remember Sally? She was in a new relationship and feeling extreme anxiety. When we explored her anxiety, we found it related to her fear of displeasing her partner and of him leaving her. Her old wire was telling her, "Keep him happy or you will be alone and won't survive."

In the beginning, intellectually, she knew this didn't make any sense, and when she said a more reasonable belief out loud, she was swamped with fear. So, we needed to start slowly. Remember, our brains give much more credence to feelings than words—think of an ingenuous apology.

Her brain was paying much more attention to her fear than to her thinking. And since the old wire was filled with fear, adding fear didn't contradict what was already there and most likely strengthened the wire.

So, Sally started by lovingly accepting and feeling compassion for right where she was—a place filled with fear that she wouldn't survive him leaving her.

Sally worked on feeling compassion for herself when these wires came up. Acceptance and compassion were contradictory or a mismatch with the feelings of fear associated with the old belief.

At the same time, she worked on paying attention to her own needs. With time, she started feeling security and pride realizing that she could take care of herself. Security and pride are examples of "reward" feelings—they generate a sense of reward in the body.

As those reward feelings strengthened, they propelled Sally forward. She felt increasing confidence in the belief that she was a strong capable woman until the time came when she no longer believed that she wouldn't be okay if he left her. She was able to notice and feel the truth of her old belief no longer making any sense.

When she could feel the truth and reward of these new beliefs, other shifts began to happen. I'll tell you more about what happened for Sally in chapter nineteen.

Sally's initial reaction to changing her wires is very common, so expect it. Remember these wires were linked with what you, at one time believed would keep you safe, and so thoughts of changing them most often evoke fear.

The idea that you can be okay even if others disagree may sound good, and it will likely generate a great deal of fear in the beginning. Because of this, it is important to match what you offer with where you are.

how to find a match

If what you say to yourself when an old assumption comes up doesn't result in some type of rewarding feeling whether it is peace, security, relief, or contentment, you are going to need to figure out what will.

What can you say or bring in that elicits feelings of reward in your body? What I mean by that is when you say it, you sigh in relief or maybe your shoulders drop down as you relax. Or maybe as you are feeling more confident, your body is more upright—standing or sitting tall with your shoulders back.

What could you say to yourself that you would believe and that would bring up a feeling of reward in your body right now, not an hour from now or tomorrow, in this moment? If you are unsure, think about what you might offer a friend who is afraid.

I mention fear as most unreasonable assumptions are fear-based although many also bring up feelings of shame. If your friend was feeling afraid or ashamed, I imagine you would be understanding and accepting of her feelings. If she deserves that kind of care, don't you as well?

If you can't *feel* compassion or acceptance, use one of the tools from the "L" step in the model—maybe bringing in someone to feel compassion for you or imagining the young part of you feeling fear or guilt and seeing if you can feel compassion for her.

Understanding and compassion originate in the thinking brain, so if you can feel compassion or understanding in this moment, you have just made a connection between the emotional brain and the thinking brain. And in a wire previously filled with fear, you have just brought in a feeling of safety.

a yellow wire turns blue

Using the image of a wire changing colors is a way I try to instill hope that starting with compassion or acceptance can make a difference, as well as why our feelings are important in changing default wiring. This is not factual neuroscience—the circuits in our brain are not different colors nor do I imagine they change color with new information.

This is simply a way of picturing a process that I bet most of you have experienced in other areas of your life. Think of something that once filled you with fear and that now you do without much fear or thought. Maybe you recall learning to drive or the first time you navigated a new program on your computer. Your feelings and beliefs changed as your level of experience changed.

To imagine this process of a wire changing color, let's use the wire that so many of my clients have uncovered, *"I'm not okay if you are unhappy with me."* Most often this is a wire filled with fear—fear of being disliked or abandoned. Let's imagine that yellow represents that fear, and because there is lots of fear, the wire is primarily filled with yellow fibers.

Because it's filled with fear, women often have a hard time feeling the truth of, *"I'm okay even if you don't think so."*

So, we start with compassion. Compassion has a very different feel to it than fear, right? For most, it brings up a feeling of security. Let's imagine secure fibers are blue. So, when that wire, filled with yellow fibers of fear, lights up, and I feel compassion for myself, I have just brought in something different—in this example a blue fiber.

One time feeling security and adding one blue fiber and the wire would still be primarily filled with yellow fear fibers, right? And if time and time again, I noticed the fear and felt compassion for myself, adding one blue fiber of security after another, the wire has the potential to change from yellow to blue.

Like my experience with dogs, as the positive interactions with dogs began to outnumber or outweigh my fears, I was able to say and believe that not all dogs are dangerous, and when I encountered a new dog, I was no longer overwhelmed by fear. And as a result, my brain stopped scanning my environment for dangerous dogs.

Likewise, when you bring enough security into a wire linking your safety with the approval of others, because you will no longer be swamped with fear, you will be able to keep your thinking brain on board and have the capability to believe that your worth is not determined by how others see you or whatever variation of that statement feels true to you.

Just like with a fear of dogs, where a certain amount of fear of unfamiliar dogs is healthy, you may feel some fear when you notice disapproval, and because you will no longer be swamped with fear, you will be able to think about whether your fear is reasonable and whether you need to heed the fear.

We don't want to totally eliminate fears of disapproval. Remember, when we no longer care what others think, we have swung over to disconnecting. And because it is so easy with this intimacy style to swing over to disconnecting when you are bringing new information into old circuits, be sure that you haven't disconnected.

Just to sum it up, the time to bring new information into an old faulty belief that you have uncovered is when that wire is "hot." And using the image of colored wires, you want to bring in a different colored wire and be sure that you can feel the truth of that information. You want to add enough of a different belief or feeling, that, figuratively speaking, you change the color of the wire.

I hope this visual metaphor has helped you picture how little steps can add up. This process also gets the thinking brain connected with these old, once-isolated wires.

the thinking brain gets involved

The more clients have been able to feel compassion and understanding when these fears about approval surfaced, the more they were forming connections between the fear wire and the thinking brain.

They were also, more often, keeping themselves from tipping into the stress response, which meant the thinking brain was staying engaged. Once the thinking brain was involved, it was like dominos falling—things started shifting quickly.

With the thinking brain engaged, women started having new awarenesses and shifts in perspectives. With time, what was once simply an intellectual understanding shifted to a felt sense of truth. As women made statements like *"That doesn't make sense. My looks don't define me."* Or *"I'm okay even if you don't approve of me,"* I could feel the truth of what they were saying.

Remember the client I mentioned in the last chapter who believed she would be abandoned if she made a mistake? She did quite a bit of emotional work tracing her feelings back to their origins, and the other thing she did was notice when this belief came up during group. When she noticed it, she felt compassion for herself for feeling that way.

As she calmed her system, she was able to observe and realize that nothing had changed in her relationships with the other group members after one of her "mistakes."

When she noticed this, she brought new information into a wire that had remained isolated in her emotional brain. Over time, she began to feel the truth of *"I can be myself, make mistakes, and be loved."*

This kind of reasoning can't happen if the wire stays isolated in our subconscious or emotional brain with no new information or connections with other parts of the brain. It also can't happen if the emotion of the wire stays predominantly fear or shame.

Because she had started feeling compassion when she noticed the shame connected with this wire, she started changing the "color" of the wire, and as a result, the wire no longer quickly triggered a stress response and a swing to disconnecting.

To change these old default wires, you need to notice them and bring in new information and feelings. To do that you have to follow through. You will also need to follow through in needs related to self-care.

We will talk about following through in part four of this chapter. For now, take some time to reflect on what you have read so far and to think about how you might apply these concepts to your own life.

in a nutshell

- If you are having trouble coming back into balance after being tipped, there may be an unreasonable assumption or belief keeping your feelings "hot."

- Most of these assumptions are out of our awareness—they are implicit memories.

- These assumptions are formed primarily in childhood when we lack the ability to look at the whole picture or put things in perspective. As a result, most are not factual.

- Without our awareness, these early conclusions made about ourselves and others became the lens through which we viewed the world.

- When these wires light up, we experience the feelings, thoughts, and body sensations that are a part of that wire. We typically assume our reactions are triggered by present situations and don't realize that we are viewing the situation through the lens of an old wire.

- To bring new more reasonable knowledge into these wires, we have to do so while they are "hot"—or when you can feel the truth of it. At the same time, or within a few hours of that time, we need to be in enough emotional balance to feel the truth of the information that contradicts the information on the wire.

- Sometimes in the beginning, it is just not possible to dispute the original belief and, in that case, you will need to start with whatever contradictory thought or emotion you can feel. For instance, you might start with compassion or acceptance for having the wire.

- It is important when you are bringing in new information, that is factual. It is easy to slip back out of balance and disconnect. One way of checking whether the information you plan to add is factual is to think about whether it would be true for your daughter or a good friend.

- Sometimes you have to stay at it, adding little bits of information or feelings that are a mismatch for those of the wire, until the time comes when you believe and feel the truth of the new factual information.

ideas for reflection

- What old, outdated assumptions have you noticed by identifying your feelings or at times when you were tipped? Write them down so you can watch for them. Identify the kinds of thoughts and feelings that come up when these wires are fired up and write them down as well. Doing so will help you notice when they are "hot" and will give you the opportunity to bring in new information.

- What is the new information that needs to come into these wires? What are the facts—not what feels true—the facts? What would you tell your daughter or a good friend?

- In stating that new information, do you believe what you are saying? Can you feel the truth or reward? If not, back up. What do you notice if you accept and feel compassion for where you are right now, even if you still believe the information on the old wire? How does your body feel when you offer yourself that caring?

chapter fifteen
part four

don't deprive yourself—follow through

In group, I would often share the following example.

"Imagine that a little boy, say around five, comes up to me and says, "I'm sad." And what if my response is, "That's nice, thanks for telling me." Then I turn away from him and go on with my day."

This example usually got a chuckle from the group members. I imagine you might be smiling as well. Intuitively, they knew this was ridiculous, and most of them would never do this to anyone, let alone a child. I imagine the same is true for you.

If you wouldn't respond in this way to someone else, don't do it to your-self. Don't check in with yourself and then leave yourself hanging! You need to follow through. Practice giving yourself what you need.

why is this important?

It is important because if you don't follow through and bring new information into your unreasonable default circuits related to approval, you will keep reinforcing them and making yourself more vulnerable to them.

And if you don't follow through with self-care, you will be more vulnerable to tipping and seeing the world from the perspective of your emotional brain—a lens that will reflect your old unreasonable expectations about yourself and others.

And there is another big benefit of following through. As you get good at identifying and meeting your needs, you will gain a sense of security.

Even if someone disappoints you, you will be there to help yourself. You can count on it. You will know what you need, and you will know whether you can either give it to yourself or whether you need to ask for help from someone else.

can I meet the need, or do I need to ask for help?

We can take care of many needs on our own. Like my need for a bath. Or if my strongest feeling was hunger, I could get something to eat. And what if your strongest feeling is sick or tired, and you have too much on your plate? Your need might be to get some help.

Or maybe you are sad, and what you need is a hug from your partner or a friend to listen to your feelings. Maybe you are angry, and you need someone to help you figure out whether you're being reasonable or to help you sort out what to do about the situation. Many times, getting some help is important in meeting our needs.

Unfortunately, asking for support is usually tough for anyone who learned this intimacy style.

You want it, that's for sure—asking for it, well that's another matter.

what—ask for what I need?

I cannot express the depth of respect I feel for my clients. I feel honored by their willingness to share and the trust they bestow on me as I witness and share in their healing journeys. In listening and working with them, I have learned so much.

I feel warmth in my heart thinking about this learning moving from one woman to the next, lightening her load, and making living a fulfilling life more than a pipe dream. I really hope this book will continue to ease women's paths and lighten their loads.

That was a bit of a digression. It came to mind when I remembered the client whose words I am about to share. Her words were the words of so many of the women working on changing this style of relating. She said, *"What? You mean I have to tell her what I need?"* She went on to say, in a somewhat sarcastic tone, *"You mean tears are running down my face, and I need to tell her I am sad?"*

This dear heart of a client grew up in a family with a strong entangled intimacy style. She was working hard to change this pattern and sharing her feelings directly went against everything she had learned about relationships. This is common.

Often women with this intimacy style believe they are communicating what they need when in fact they are sharing what is happening for them with the expectation that their partner, friend, or whoever, will intuit what they need.

Let's go back to Nancy. Remember Nancy longed for a committed relationship? Instead, her relationships often ended when she got tired of giving and lost her temper.

When I asked Nancy whether she had shared her wishes with her partners, she told me she had. Nancy said that she let the men she was dating know *"she was tired"* or that her day *"had been a rough one."*

Nancy added, *"I don't know what is wrong with these guys I pick. They don't seem to get it."* She went on to say, *"I mean, if I told my sister that I'd had a rough day, she would surprise me with something nice or maybe take me out for supper."*

She asked, *"Why don't these men do something like that?"*

This is a great example of the entangled intimacy style in action. Nancy expected the men she was dating would intuit that she needed something from them by her letting them know she had a hard day.

Do you see yourself in this example? Do you share your feelings with someone and hope or expect them to do something?

Nancy's sister grew up in the same household. They were both good at intuiting people's needs and trying to "make" them happy.

Let's take a moment to look more closely at the desire in this intimacy style for others to intuit our needs.

if you love me, you will know what I need

A huge stumbling block for women with an entangled intimacy style in asking for help is the belief that they shouldn't have to ask. If you love me, you will know what I need. Can you relate? If so, you aren't alone.

For most women with this intimacy style, it just plain feels wrong to ask for what they want or need.

I'm imagining that the ability to anticipate other people's needs was a skill that once kept us safe when our safety depended upon being chosen by a mate and that over time, this connection between anticipating needs and safety has morphed into a belief about what it means to be loved. As a result, when women think about asking for what they need it brings up fears of not being loved.

Another hard part about changing this belief is that women are often in caretaking roles, raising children or caring for aging parents. Getting good at anticipating needs comes in handy as a caretaker. Because women often spend a great deal of time in these roles anticipating other people's needs, there is an expectation that others will do the same for them.

anticipating needs ≠ love

Let's go back to my client's question about whether I was suggesting that she needed to tell her partner that she was sad and needed a hug when she was crying.

The answer is "yes." It may seem obvious to you that your tears would communicate that you are sad and need a hug, and unless you have previously shared with the other person your specific needs, any number of interpretations are possible. I bet there are many of you reading this who cry for reasons other than sadness. I expect quite a few of you cry in anger, and I don't imagine you feel like a hug when you're angry.

And if you have this wiring and your partner misses the mark, it will likely trigger feelings of being unloved. For these reasons, it is going to be important to notice when this wire connecting anticipating what you need and love has been triggered and to bring in some new, more factual, information.

It is totally understandable that you want people to notice what is important to you, and I hope they do. And their ability to do that has to be disconnected from how much they love you or your worth.

You are not unlovable or unloved if someone you care about doesn't correctly anticipate your needs. These are two separate things—one does not equal the other.

You have a much better chance of getting what you need if you let people know what it is you need! Working on the unreasonable assumption linking love with anticipating your needs will put you in a better place to start voicing your needs.

And, yes, you must say it out loud, not simply give hints. And you're going to need to break the habit of communicating when you are past your limits.

communicate when you are calm

Checking in to be sure you are in the middle is important before deciding what you need, and it is also important in communication. So, before speaking up, be sure that you and the other person are calm and in emotional balance. In doing this, consider your physical well-being. If you are too tired, sick, or in pain, you will likely be in the stress response.

Being sure you are in emotional balance is crucial. And as I shared with you a couple of sections ago, this can be tricky. If you are tipped, it will likely feel imperative that you communicate right this minute. If someone's life is in danger, go for it. If you feel you can't wait another moment to talk about the laundry on the floor, you are most likely tipped and anything you say will probably come out in a disconnecting way. I know it is hard, and if you can, wait.

Remember, disconnecting is the default response in this intimacy style. When you can't take it anymore, you find some way to escape, or you communicate with little caring for how it will be received—like the striking of a snake, using my client's words.

This is what Nancy did, and it left her riddled with guilt and fear or devastated because it ended her relationships. Waiting until you are at your limit to communicate will rarely get you what you want.

The time to communicate is when you are calm and in the middle. The place where you are connected with your own needs and feel warmhearted compassion for the needs of the other person.

In the middle, you will also have access to all of the resources of the thinking brain.

Resources like:

- Perspective: being able to think of the pros and cons of what you are about to say and understanding the other person's perspective
- Planning: coming up with a plan for what to say or ask for
- Compassion: for yourself and the other person

If you are tipped, with the more primitive parts of your brain running the show, it will feel like you against them. It will be impossible to see the gray—to see that there could be some good in both perspectives.

You have the best chance of feeling "heard" when you can think, plan, take perspective, and feel compassion. And this boils down to being in balance, so your entire brain is on board. It boils down to being in the middle, the place of "both/and."

As I mentioned earlier, a simple test to see whether you are in balance is to check to see whether you feel warmhearted compassion for the other person and whether you can truly understand their perspective. Compassion and understanding require the thinking brain, and so if you can't do this, you are too tipped to be communicating.

It is also important that you choose a time when you think the person you are about to communicate with is in balance for the same reasons.

preparing to speak up

These questions will help you ensure you are in the middle and will get you ready to communicate your needs. Even if you never say a word, this is a great practice. It will help you learn about being in the middle. Ask yourself:

- How am I feeling right now?...*and*...How is the other person feeling?
- What do I need?...*and*...What might they need?
- What is my perspective?...*and*...What is their perspective?
- Can I hold onto what I need *and* feel empathy for their needs?

This practice has several payoffs. It will help you

- Put your feelings into words.
- Realize that you are a separate being from the other person, who has differing needs.
- And most importantly, realize that you can care about others, and they can care about you, and you can disagree.

making a request

When you make a request, it is important to communicate feelings of warmheartedness, compassion, or empathy; to keep both wheels turning, and to be specific. Let's take a moment to consider each of those components.

warmhearted compassion, empathy, respect, or love

When you are ready to communicate your feelings, before you speak, take a moment to connect with warmth, caring, empathy, love, or compassion for yourself and the other person. Think about whether there is a way you can communicate, verbally or non-verbally, these feelings or an understanding of their perspective.

As we talked about earlier, our brains give more credence to tone and expressions than to words, so you must be honestly feeling what you are expressing for it to be felt and believed by the other person.

specific, one need at a time

When you are making a request, make it specific. Express what you feel and what you need. Use "I" statements in doing this. For instance, *"I feel sad today and need a hug. Would you be up for giving me one?"*

Keep your sentences short and to the point. Avoid lengthy explanations and especially avoid blaming. Remember we are each responsible for our own feelings. Think about how it feels to hear "I feel sad," and "You made me sad."

Hearing those two statements feels different, doesn't it? How do you feel when you hear "I feel sad"? Do you feel pulled in and want to hear more? How about "You made me sad"? Do you notice yourself starting to think about what you might have done or possibly getting ready to defend yourself?

If the other person is thinking about how to defend themself, it will be hard for them to listen. You have a much better chance of getting what you need by talking about your feelings and needs. And it is important to keep the cart rolling.

the two-wheeled cart

What we've really been talking about in these last few sections is keeping both wheels turning on the cart of your relationship. And it can be a good way of reminding yourself of how to stay in the middle. Remember that both wheels need to be in place and turning to keep the relationship moving forward.

Check to be sure your wheel is on your side of the cart, that you have checked in with how you feel and what you need, and that you are allowing the other person's wheel to move freely on their side of the cart. By that I mean you have considered how they are feeling, what they might need, and their perspective on the situation.

Are you allowing them to be an individual and to blossom and grow in the same way you are hoping to blossom? Ask rather than expect. Consider using questions like, "Would you be willing to...?" Remember, what they decide is about them and not a reflection of your worth. Let me give you an example.

it didn't work

One night in my women's group, as women were sharing how their week had gone, one member looked "down." When I asked her what she was feeling she said she felt sad, as she had tried making a request and it hadn't worked. What she meant was that the other person hadn't agreed to her request. This is a common place to end up for anyone with this intimacy style.

Why? Because making a request is going to light up one of the core wires of this intimacy style. "If you know what will make me happy, you should do it." Now my client didn't realize at first that a core wire had been triggered. She believed that the way she made the request hadn't worked — *if she would have asked correctly, he would have agreed.*

When we explored why she believed he would have agreed if she asked in an effective way, she shared that it had to be something about her or what she was doing because *"when you love someone you give them what they need."* And there it was — the core expectation connecting love with giving someone what they need or want to keep them happy.

This core assumption was leading her to believe that the problem was with her or her ability to ask for what she needed. If you love me and know what I need and didn't give it to me, I must have done something wrong, or I must not be lovable. Does this sound familiar? Do you believe that when you don't get what you need the problem is with you?

It is so interesting how all the core assumptions of this intimacy style seem to work their way back to a sense of not being good enough. My client believed her request wasn't good enough and that if she was "good enough," her husband would have granted her request.

When you make a request, your default wiring is going to lead you to expect the other person to grant your request, and if they don't, painful feelings are likely to come up. This is where connection with your feelings is going to help you.

Being disappointed when you make a request is an opportunity. It will likely be uncomfortable, and you can use those uncomfortable feelings to identify the assumption that is hiding under the discomfort. While this wire is "hot" or lit up, you have the chance to bring in some new information or connect it with the thinking brain even if it is through acceptance or compassion.

This is your chance to start changing this old wiring that is keeping you reactive to the responses of others.

Contrary to what your wiring leads you to believe, just because the other person knows what would make you happy doesn't mean they are going to give it to you. They may, or they may not.

And this is what needs rewiring: *their response has nothing to do with how much they care about you.* And *their reactions mean nothing about you as a person.* Those are their feelings.

The other person can choose not to do something you want them to do and still care deeply about you. This may disappoint you. You may feel sad, and it doesn't mean they don't love you or that you are unlovable.

responsibility for feelings

This seems like it might be a good time to spend a bit more time talking about responsibility for feelings because almost everyone struggles with this concept, and this is going to be an essential piece of the new information that needs to come into those old, entangled intimacy wires.

I hope that the following example will help. It is the one I often share with clients trying to untangle the belief that they can "make" people feel a certain way.

Imagine I am a supervisor who has called three of my employees into my office to inform them of some changes I want them to make. After I finish, they head to the break room. The first employee says, *"I am livid! How dare she reprimand us in front of each other. She's an idiot!"*

The second employee doesn't say anything and is thinking, *"I'm such a screwup. Why can't I do anything right? I'm feeling so down right now."*

And the third employee says, *"Whew! I'm so relieved, I thought for a moment she was going to let us go, and instead, we just need to change a few things."*

I said the same words to all three employees at the same time and in the same place. The emotion that came up for each of them was different: anger, sadness, and relief. I couldn't possibly have caused those emotions. Right?

The same thing could happen if I commented on appearance. One person might feel angry that I commented on her appearance, another might have a wire about worth get triggered and feel afraid, and yet another might be wondering, "I wonder what led her to comment on my appearance?" and so be feeling curious.

Emotions come from inside each of us. They come from whatever meaning we attach to what is happening and from whatever wires the brain matches with the current experience. No matter what we do, we can't guarantee another person will feel a certain way or do the same for us as we would do for them.

You may have a hard time believing this, and that's okay. It's okay to be where you are with any of this. I've had clients say to me, *"I know I have heard that a hundred times, and for the first time, I really get it."* This is the reason that you may have noticed that I repeat or come back to ideas I have presented earlier in the book. Different ideas "click" at different times for different people.

The old wiring is strong, and it pulls you right back to the old way of doing and believing. The more you practice with the steps and think about what I am sharing with you, the easier it will be to step off the old wires and have a new understanding.

Be patient and be kind—in the same way that you would be with someone else who is trying to learn something new.

The next thing I want to address in this "offer" section is saying "no" because it is often the hardest thing to communicate for those with this style of relating.

saying "no"

A big part of offering yourself what you need is learning to say "no." Many people struggle with setting limits and being assertive about their needs. And if you have learned this style of relating to others, your struggles with being assertive may differ from those without this style of relating.

The unconscious wiring of this intimacy style pulls women into the needs of others while losing awareness of their own needs. Many people with this style aren't even aware they don't want to do something when they agree to do it.

Remember Madeline who supervised a group of women employees? Madeline would connect so deeply with the experiences of her employees that she often found herself doing their work over the weekend.

This had less to do with her ability to say "no" and more to do with how absorbed she became in her employees' difficulties. She could feel how hard it must be to be in their shoes.

Without her realizing it, her wiring pushed her to believe that "she should" help them. In the moment, she wasn't the least bit aware of what this would mean for her.

Her employees loved her. They felt truly cared about and that their needs mattered. And Madeline's needs got lost in the shuffle, and she felt exhausted from working so many weekends trying to keep everything running at the office.

It wasn't that Madeline didn't know how to say "no;" saying "no" wasn't in her awareness. The same was true for Margaret, who often found her schedule overbooked despite her need to find time to relax. She often scheduled time for coffee or lunch with friends and ended up dreading these get-togethers.

As soon as a friend suggested getting together, Margaret started feeling guilty and fearful about declining. Her unconscious wiring was telling her that her friends would no longer consider her a "good friend," so she would say "yes," and she would listen as if she had all the time and energy in the world.

Both Margaret and Madeline were strong, capable women. They weren't pushovers. They weren't shy. What they had was a *powerful unconscious force driving them to pay attention to the needs of others at the expense of their own.*

keeping your finger on the pulse of your inner life

To change that pattern, Margaret and Madeline had to make that unconscious wiring conscious so they could work with it. They had to start monitoring what was happening inside of them to do things differently.

You most likely already do this with the people in your life. Think about how you do this in other relationships—maybe with your partner or your coworkers. I imagine you notice subtle signs that something is amiss and try to take some action to remedy it.

We are simply applying this skill to your self-care. The goal is to catch the old wires that keep you from saying no and to bring some new information into them. This will also help you to notice what is happening inside before you are so over-tired or frustrated that you are ready to disconnect in some way.

To keep yourself from swinging from appeasing to disconnecting, it is going to be important for you to stay connected with the part of you who feels your feelings and the question, "Will agreeing to this stress or overwhelm her?"

And, if the answer is "yes," and what you are about to do will stress her, this is your chance to be her advocate. If it is hard to say "no" for yourself, could you say it for her?

dealing with the fear of saying no

If fear comes up in advocating for her or yourself, imagine the part of you feeling afraid standing in front of you.

As she is standing there "shaking in her boots," ask,

- What are you afraid of? Help her put it in a short sentence. "I feel afraid that..."

- What is she assuming will happen if she doesn't agree?

- Is she afraid that she won't be loved or that she will be abandoned if she doesn't say "yes?"

Look for unreasonable assumptions in what she is saying. If what she is saying sounds reasonable, you are most likely merging with her and "on the wire" of the old fear. If so, to get your thinking brain engaged, ask yourself,

- What do I know now that I didn't know as a child?

- What would I tell a friend who was afraid to say "no?"

- Would I encourage a friend to say "no" if she needed to?

Let the scared part of you know that she has the right to say "no." Let her know that she will be lovable even if she disappoints others. Let her know that you will be there to support her even if others choose to leave. Make sure that she understands that their choice to leave is theirs and not the result of what she says or does. Let her know that she will be okay because you will be there loving her. As you do that, put your hand on your heart. Feel support coming from you to you.

And as you feel that support, see if you can also open yourself up to the support and love that surrounds you. Feel the support from those who love you—from the spiritual, your entelechy, and from the universe.

you don't need to explain

My clients often find themselves offering long explanations for why they are saying "no." You don't need to do this. You don't need to justify your decision. If you can't or don't want to do something, saying "no" is sufficient. It is your choice.

Likewise, the other person has a right to their feelings. If they feel disappointed, feeling disappointed is about them. Remember, their feelings are their feelings and not a reflection of you or of their degree of caring for you.

They can be disappointed, and you can still say "no." Your job is to stay in the middle and not disconnect even when the answer is not the one you hoped to get.

Who you are and how much you care are not determined by how much you give. You may want to put that on your mirror as a reminder. And if you keep giving beyond your limits, something will fall apart. It may be your health or the relationship. It is better for both you and the other person to be clear about what you can and cannot do.

Remember Nancy who gave and gave in relationships until she was exhausted and resentful? When she communicated her needs from a place of exhaustion and anger, it often ended the relationship, and she was left feeling guilty and lonely.

Nancy later realized that she could have saved herself and her partners grief by being able to say "no" rather than giving past her limits.

be prepared

Because the invisible force of this intimacy style will pull you to appease or disconnect when you are near the other person, it is helpful to practice saying the words you would like to say before you say them to the other person. Write down what you plan to say and read your words out loud. How would you feel if you heard that request? Would you understand, specifically, what the person wants from you? Can you feel their caring?

Once you feel secure that both wheels are turning in making your request, take time to practice, either in your imagination or out loud. Practice what you will do when fear generated from your old wires comes up and potentially derails you. Imagine noticing the fear and giving yourself what you need to follow through.

Writing it down may also help to remind you of your plan. You might write something on a card to carry in your purse or put a note on your phone to remind you that your needs matter and to *be an advocate for the feeler of your feelings* when fear comes up around doing things differently. Here are some ideas you might include in your reminder.

- What people think or how they react to me doesn't determine my worth.
- People can be disappointed with me and care deeply for me.
- I'm not responsible for other people's feelings. I am responsible for my own feelings. I can't control other people's feelings—only my own.
- I can care, and I can't keep people happy.
- If I no longer care how others feel, I have slipped out of the middle and have disconnected.
- Keeping people happy does not equal love.

- How well others anticipate my needs is not a measure of their caring or of my worth.
- I can't keep giving when I have nothing left to give.
- I can't help others if I'm too tired, anxious, or depressed from over-giving.
- You could use Madeline's question, "How full is my tank?" I will share more about that in a later chapter.
- You might also remind yourself that the way you have been doing it doesn't work.
- Write down whatever you have learned from this book that will help you jump off that old wire that pulls you to look for approval from others and that will help you to think about love and connection in a new way.
- And remind yourself that you get to choose.

you get to choose

The goal of this work is to make informed choices rather than being at the mercy of the automatic responses generated by old default wiring. When your thinking brain is onboard, choice is possible, whereas when a default circuit is running the show, you are along for the ride.

There are times when it will be important to bow to social pressures or to choose to do what others want to do even when it is not what you would like to do. This is part of maintaining connection and the give and take of relationships. You may also choose to give when you are totally overwhelmed and exhausted.

It is always your choice. There is no "right" or "wrong" in this.

They are your choices to make. The important part is that you make a choice rather than letting your default wiring pull you into appeasing or disconnecting.

And for those of you who find yourself automatically saying "yes" and later regretting it, you might need to come up with a plan to buy yourself some time. For instance, you might get into the practice of saying, "Let me get back to you on that."

Making a choice is empowering. Feeling like you have to do something can leave you feeling like a victim.

the power of choice

An entangled intimacy style can foster a sense of victimhood. I don't say that in a judging way. What I mean is that when we are appeasing, it feels like there is so much that we "have to do." We have to look a certain way, dress a certain way, have our house be a certain way, and then there is getting all the people in our life to approve of us. As a result, we can feel like victims of our circumstances.

Even if you struggle changing your patterns or even if you decide not to make changes in your pattern of appeasing, how you view your experiences can make a big difference in how you feel. Here's what I mean by that.

Remember when I was doing all that shoveling without any help? And all the anger that came up until I got myself back into balance and realized that it was my choice to shovel?

My realization that I had made the choice to shovel totally changed my experience. I could have waited and hired someone, and I didn't want to do that.

In reality, we make choices with everything we do. Sometimes, none of our choices are that great; we are choosing the lesser of two difficult situations, and we are still choosing.

Our use of language, once again, is deceiving. In this case, it supports our powerlessness. Or as my clients have shared, *"I have to work." "I have to pick up the kids from school." "I have to fix dinner."*

The "have to" gives the sense that there is no choice. Now, I'm imagining that you are thinking, as my clients have, *"I don't have a choice. I have to work, pick up kids, and fix dinner."*

I get that it feels that way, and the truth is that you are choosing to do those things because you like the outcome or because there is less pain involved with that choice.

You could choose not to work, right? You could live on the street or try to find someone to take care of you. I'm imagining you like the benefits of working, so you choose to work. It feels very different to say, "I choose to work because I like the benefits of working" rather than "I have to work."

Your kids could find their way home on their own, and you probably choose to pick them up so that you are sure that they get home safely.

Can you feel the difference? Give yourself the chance to feel the strength that comes from knowing it is your choice.

imagination and intention

Before winding up this chapter, I want to remind you to make use of your imagination and positive intentions to help prime your brain for the changes you want for yourself. Remember the studies I shared earlier with you in which people changed the structure of their brains using only their imaginations?

No matter where you are in the process, use imagination and positive intention to your advantage as you work on changing the impact that approval has on how you feel about yourself.

If you are working on loving acceptance and self-compassion, imagine yourself at the finish line. What will it be like when you are there—when you freely offer yourself compassion? Imagine it with all your senses and feel what it will be like to be the recipient of all that care you have been sharing with others. Experience the reward—feel it in your body.

As you work with your imagination, remember, it is important for your feelings to match your thoughts or to have a clear intention paired with a positive emotion.[72] So be clear about what you want and imagine yourself in your desired outcome and feel the reward of being there.

As you begin your day, set the intention of keeping your finger on the pulse of your inner life. Feel what it is like to be so connected with your inner life that you notice feelings when they are small and give yourself what you need before you have tipped into the stress response. Feel the reward of receiving this type of responsive care.

See yourself noticing any signs of the old unreasonable assumptions which link your worth with approval and taking that opportunity to bring new information into those wires. Notice how it feels to be moving through your day catching any thoughts or feelings related to the old assumption that would likely throw you out of balance and instead bringing in reasonable, factual information. Feel the strength, confidence, or pride that comes from trusting your own wisdom rather than looking to others for a measure of how well you are doing.

And if fear comes up in imagining any of these steps, remember, this is *your* imagination. You can design it in any way that will help make it easier for you to reach your goal. What would you need to make it easier?

Maybe you start by imagining yourself surrounded by supportive people when you speak up, or that people are cheering you on as you voice your opinion or walk on the beach wearing the suit that you've been putting off wearing until you have lost weight. Feel the reward of that until it is solid. When you've got that down, make it a bit harder.

Maybe you voice your opinion, and someone rolls their eyes. What would help you deal with that? Would it help to imagine a supportive friend there with you or maybe your entelechy or a spiritual figure reminding you that you are meant to be you in this life?

Use what works for you and helps you experience the reward of being yourself. Start to lay down some tracks in your brain so that when the situation arises in real life your brain will already have a path to follow.

Remember the brain doesn't differentiate between what is actually happening and what we are vividly imagining. Use this to your advantage. Spend as much time as you can in the future you desire for yourself when it comes to separating your worth from the approval of others and feel all the rewards of being there.

give yourself time

I have shared a great deal of information with you in this chapter. I hope you have taken your time with it. I'd like to nudge you to go back and read it again, taking time to practice the skills, either now or after finishing the book.

It took time and practice for my clients to incorporate these skills into their lives. I imagine the same will be true for you. Give yourself that time.

Mastery of skills sneaks up on us. Think of something you learned in the past and how in the beginning it was hard, or maybe felt impossible, and then at some point suddenly you were doing it without thinking about it. My clients often worried they weren't making progress in the beginning and then at some point, were surprised by how much had shifted.

As with most things in life, the more time you spend with these skills the easier and more natural they will become. Remember your brain will begin to help you with the process by creating structures to support whatever you are practicing with regularity.

And if you are having trouble getting started with the skills or making your practice consistent, please don't be hard on yourself or get discouraged. You may simply need more exposure and the chance to be guided in using the skills rather than just reading about them. I created the online companion course to help you with that. I share more about the course in the "where to go from here" section on page 361 or you can learn more here: <u>bit.ly/neverenoughonline</u>.

in a nutshell

- Following through and giving yourself what you need is important in maintaining emotional balance as well as in changing old wiring linking approval with your self-worth.

- If you don't follow through and bring something new into the wires, you will simply reinforce what is already there, making them stronger.

- An important part of caring for yourself is asking for support when you need it. Women with this style of relating often express thoughts or feelings rather than a specific request for help. As a result, women many times don't get what they want or need.

- In this intimacy style, intuiting needs is seen as a measure of love or caring. Because most people are not mind-readers, women often end up feeling undervalued or unloved.

- When you make a request, the response you receive to your request is not a measure of the degree of caring the person has for you. It also means nothing about you as a person or your worth. Their responses reflect them and not you.

- When you check in and realize you need help:

> Ask directly and with a warm heart—keeping both your needs and the needs of the other person in mind, as you do so.
>
> If you can't honestly *feel* compassion, empathy, or respect for the other person, you have most likely swung over to disconnecting. Getting yourself back into the middle will give you a much better chance of being heard and not damaging the relationship.

- For most women with this intimacy style, saying "no" isn't even on their radar due to the powerful force to appease or disconnect, and contemplating saying "no" often brings up fear.
- Be prepared to deal with the fear that is likely going to come up when you speak up or say "no." Mentally rehearse how you will deal with that fear.
- Give yourself the chance to choose—making a choice feels empowering. It is a different experience choosing to give or help than it is to feel you must.
- You are working on changing old wires related to safety. There may be both resistance and fear as you do this work. Be kind and gentle with yourself.
- And remember to use the resource of your imagination. The brain doesn't differentiate between imagination and real life, so spend as much time as possible "living" in the future you desire for yourself and feeling the reward of doing so.
- If fear comes up in your imagination, remember it is *your*

imagination, so you can adjust outcomes and participants in any way that will help you feel empowered and rewarded.

- If you are struggling with incorporating the skills into your life or remembering to practice them, please don't be hard on yourself. You may just need more exposure and the chance to be guided in using the skills rather than just reading about them. I created the online companion course to help you with that. I will share more in the "where to go from here" section, or you can also learn more here: <u>bit.ly/neverenoughonline</u>.

I'm sending you a big hug!

ideas for reflection

- How has it been to give yourself what you need? What feelings have come up around doing this?
- What reactions come up in thinking about communicating a request?
- When you think about saying "no," do you notice any core assumptions about yourself or about what would happen if you disagreed?
- What is a small step you could take to begin communicating

what you need or in saying "no" when a request is not in your best interest?

- Take time to feel love and compassion for yourself. Wherever you are in this process, it is right for you in the present moment and means nothing about what is possible in the future.

chapter sixteen

"M": moving on to what brings you joy and allows you to bloom

You have now learned how to bring your attention back to yourself with loving compassion, how to use this awareness to better care for yourself, and how to bring new information into old wires that have been keeping you vulnerable to the reactions of others.

The purpose of the "M" step is to align yourself with your passions and larger purpose in this life. Why purpose? Because having purpose helps to buffer you from the ups and downs of life. Writing that reminds me of the saying "keep your eyes on the prize."

Who would you be if you weren't spending your time trying to keep people happy and if it didn't matter whether people approved of you? This is the question for the "M" step in the BLOOM model.

This is the moment you've been waiting for. Now that you are separating your worth from the opinions of others, who will you be, and what will you do?

The "M" in BLOOM is about connecting with your inner wisdom and the larger purpose for your life. Who did you come into this world to be? What are your deepest desires?

I'm imagining you've had very little time to give this much thought. All of your attention has been going outward toward others and things that you thought would bring approval or keep people happy with you.

Each time you observe how you are feeling and what you need, you can learn more about who you are, what is important to you, and what brings you joy. It will help you connect with your internal wisdom and a roadmap that is yours alone.

Checking in helped me to clarify my purpose—my desire to support others, especially women, in celebrating their uniqueness, feeling more secure in being themselves, and tapping into their own wisdom. Narrowing the focus of my work to align it with my purpose has exponentially increased the joy I feel in my work.

Because my work now aligns with my passion and purpose, I am able to use my natural gifts rather than trying to be good at everything and constantly being reminded of my shortcomings.

What is your purpose?

I also discovered a source of joy I had no idea was there—a love of color and working with color. I never would have imagined color would bring me so much joy. Now creating beauty is a big part of my life, whether that is in gardening or the colors I choose for my house or the clothes I wear. Working with color fills me with joy.

What brings you joy?

Are there skills or talents you have allowed to go dormant because you felt criticized or because you didn't feel supported by the people in your life?

Asking you this reminds me of Samantha.

Samantha

Samantha struggled with fear generated from a belief that she never *"measured up."* Her body was too big, her house was too messy, she would lose and forget things. She was constantly worrying that she was disappointing people, especially her husband.

In sitting with Samantha, I sensed she was an artist at heart. She oozed creativity. Yet Samantha worked really hard to fight those creative tendencies. She tried to *"stay between the lines"* rather than be the expansive person she was meant to be in the world. She tried to be *"orderly"* like her husband. And she expected her body to be *"between the lines"* of social expectations.

The more Samantha checked in and felt compassion for herself, the more she embraced the truth of who she was. Samantha was one who loved the idea of entelechy—knowing that the wisdom of the universe was supporting her to be herself. She used that concept as a source of support as she began stepping out into the world as herself. There was great freedom in this. She no longer spent most of her time tipped out of balance and turning to food for comfort.

She also started giving herself a break when it came to misplacing things. She realized that being creative meant she had a lot of things going at one time, making it easy to misplace things.

Samantha started dancing and listening to music rather than pushing herself to exercise in ways that felt like torture. Her image for letting her true self shine was driving down the highway with the radio blaring and her hair flying in the wind.

Samantha realized that all of her striving to be someone she wasn't had led to her feeling depressed and to overeating. And when she overate, she felt guilty and more stressed about her body. It was a vicious cycle.

In what ways are you similar to Samantha?

Are you caught in a vicious cycle of one sort or another, trying to keep people happy and feeling stressed, depressed, or anxious? Who, and how, are you meant to be in the world? When you connect with your entelechy, the wisest part of yourself, your higher power or the spiritual, what do you sense about your life's purpose? I'm hoping that reading this book and practicing the BLOOM model help you connect with your inner wisdom and that your wisdom, as well as your connection with larger sources of support, will guide you in creating a life that is yours and yours alone.

a rose isn't meant to be an orchid

This seems obvious, doesn't it? And yet how often do we as women try to be something we aren't and never can be.

Just as a rose seed is destined to be a rose and not an orchid, you are destined to be who you were meant to be, not who or what someone else wants you to be or thinks you should be.

No matter how much a rose might be told she should be more like an orchid, a rose is going to be a rose. If I am disappointed with the rose because it is not an orchid and don't take care of it, it will still be a rose, and it won't be the healthy beautiful rose it could be with loving care.

In the same way, striving to be what you think others want you to be can lead you away from your self-care and prevent you from becoming all that you could and are meant to be—a role only you can play in this world.

As Archbishop Desmond Tutu shares in his conversations with His Holiness the Dali Lama and Douglas Abrams in *The Book of Joy,* *"No one is a divine accident."* And Douglas Abrams adds, *"While we may not be special, we are essential. No one can fulfill our role but us in the divine plan or karmic unfolding."*[73]

All the work you have done so far in this book has helped to build a connection with yourself and your needs. Doing this puts you in touch with your internal compass. And when we stop, connect, and feel compassion and love for ourselves and others, it also seems to open us up to truly feeling love and guidance from others, as well as from larger sources of support like from the spiritual or from the universe.

The more you connect with your inner wisdom, the clearer the path will become and the more supported you will feel.

As you connect with your internal wisdom and compass, feel the universe ready to support you in your becoming. Just as the energy of the universe supports a rose seed in becoming a gorgeous rose, the energy is there to support you in being the most radiant version of yourself.

What is your North Star? This is the moment to align yourself with your purpose.

Life will soon pull you back in with all of its busyness. Take this moment to connect with your purpose and your greatest desire for this life.

Write it down. What does it look like? What does it feel like?

What would someone notice if they saw you in this greatest vision for yourself? "Paint a picture" using all your senses and with as much detail as possible. Use your imagination to be in that experience and to feel the rewards of being in this greatest vision for yourself.

If you are unsure, ask for guidance from larger sources of support and insight, like your entelechy, God, the spiritual or source energy—whatever matches your values and beliefs. Spend time in quiet reflection or in prayer to create the space to receive this guidance.

When you have connected with your purpose, what is one step you could take right now that would move you closer to your vision for your life?

This is the moment to take that step!

in a nutshell

- Now that you have created space for yourself, this is the moment to move toward your passions. To move toward what brings you joy. To take a step that will bring you closer to your destiny—to your North Star.

- Just as there is an entelechy supporting a rose seed to become a rose, there is also an entelechy or life force in the universe supporting you to be you.

- Feel the universe supporting you and cheering you on, supporting you to be all that you can and were meant to be in this life.

ideas for reflection

- What brings you joy?

- What is your passion? Your greater purpose? Your North Star?

- Take some time to reflect and either write about or illustrate your larger purpose or your destiny—really "paint the picture" with your words or with what you draw.

- What do you notice when you think about and or paint the picture of your larger purpose? Do any painful feelings come up, like fear or guilt? If so, look for an unreasonable assumption beneath these feelings.

- Mentally rehearse the experience of your destiny or larger purpose. Be in the experience, making sure to feel the reward feelings that you will be feeling as you align with your greater purpose.

- What is a first step you will take, no matter how small, to move you closer to your destiny?

part three

what your journey might look like

chapter seventeen
there will be bumps— okay, maybe even some mountains

Now you have a plan and the acronym BLOOM to remind you of the steps. The steps and process might sound simple, and I know from experience, both mine and that of my clients, that this process sounds easier than it is.

Remember that default wiring that we talked about? You are going to be trying to interrupt that wiring. Your brain is going to want to continue with business as usual. So, any one step might be difficult. I am not sharing this with you to scare you or to be discouraging. What I don't want is for you to take it personally or to be hard on yourself if you find the work of the model difficult.

You may find it hard to bring your attention back to yourself, let alone notice what is happening inside you. You might have a very negative reaction to even thinking about being compassionate with yourself.

And if this is your intimacy style, you are up against wiring that has been in place for years and is most likely wired in a way that your brain associates with safety.

there will be resistance

Our brains are reluctant to let go of anything connected or wired with safety. Expect this. Keep practicing with the steps of the model. If fear comes up, the more loving and accepting you can be in face of the fear, the more chance you have of changing the emotional valence of those wires.

Fear begets more fear. Love and compassion calm fear. Do your best to just keep moving forward with as much love and compassion as you can muster, expecting to run into bumps along the way.

One bump you may run into is the bump of seeing this style of relating, or your need for approval, everywhere in your life.

"it's everywhere I turn!"

This is a pretty predictable reaction. You may go from not even being aware of this style of relating to seeing it everywhere. A client this week expressed how discouraged she was feeling about seeing signs of her entangled intimacy style so often in her life. She said:

"I have always seen myself as a good communicator, and now that I see this entangled style everywhere I turn, I am starting to question that."

First, we realized that she was in the stress response, and because of that, she was seeing things in an "either/or" kind of way. In reality, her entangled style wasn't "everywhere" and because she had this style didn't mean she wasn't a good communicator. In the stress response, her emotional brain was overgeneralizing.

In fact, this woman is an excellent communicator. A big part of her success at work has been the result of her communication skills, especially her writing. And when she is in a relationship, these wires tend to light up.

Recognizing the both/and—she has a tendency to appease or to defer to the needs of others in relationships, and she is a good communicator—helped her to come back into balance. She realized that her tendency to appease was simply a wire and not a reflection of her totality.

I shared with her how common it is for women to get discouraged when they notice the prevalence of this pattern. This, too, seemed to help. This was an advantage of being in my women's group.

Members could see that there were other women—talented, capable women—also struggling with deferring to the needs or preferences of others (appeasing), and then pulling away through words or actions when they felt "over it" (disconnecting).

It was helpful for them to hear how often these women they cared for and respected were swayed by the reactions of others.

That is one of the reasons that I have shared with you so many client examples.

I hope the examples have helped you realize:

- You aren't alone.

- Other capable, intelligent women share these patterns.
- This is just one part of the totality of you.
- When you feel like it defines you, you are most likely in the stress response and as a result, viewing yourself in an all-or-nothing way.

there may be resistance to your growth

For the most part, my clients have been pleasantly surprised by the reactions of others when they started taking better care of themselves and directly communicated their needs. Most times, people in their lives were happy to know how to help them rather than having to guess.

And sometimes this wasn't true.

Remember Olivia, who felt she was too big to be outside enjoying the activities she loved and excelled in? One of the obstacles Olivia faced in accepting herself was her husband's reactions. He knew that she had been coming to counseling for help with her eating, and he expected that she would lose weight as a result. She knew he was disappointed that she hadn't lost weight.

It took time, and Olivia was able to hold onto her truth about what was good for her body *and* accept her husband's disappointment.

She did quite a bit of soul-searching and reading and realized that accepting her body was much better for her health than the restrictive eating she had been doing to maintain a thinner body. You'll learn more about the changes Olivia made in the next chapter.

And it is useful to realize that as you work on separating your worth from approval, you may very well face resistance from the outside. You may feel pressure from those in your life, as well as from society in general.

By society in general, I'm referring to messages from the media or from your social group which may go against what you have determined is best for you.

Remember to use the steps of the BLOOM model to help you deal with these pressures. Keep checking in with the feeling part of you and be sure that you are being her advocate. As you do that, try your best to stay in the middle, keeping both your needs and the needs of others in your awareness—remembering that both wheels need to turn for the cart to move forward.

And also remember that the other person's reaction doesn't determine your worth. Those are simply their feelings and their reactions. If you are feeling pressure to meet societal standards for appearance, take a moment to recall the big industries that are likely driving those standards. Take a trip to the shopping mall or grocery store to get a more reasonable idea of the size and shapes of women's bodies, as well as the clothes they wear.

And remember that reactions always have more to do with the person reacting than the person the reaction is directed toward. If I tell you that I like your hair, my comment is a reflection of my preferences and most likely represents some worry in me that brought my attention to your hair.

As I have shared with you the brain will pull us to notice things that have been a concern. I will share more about this in a bit. And, if I worry about my weight, it is likely I will notice how much you weigh.

This is another reason that using other's approval as a measure of your worth is so problematic. A comment about your weight can send you into a downward spiral when in reality, the comment is a reflection of the speaker's own concerns and isn't really about you.

If this is a hard concept, think back to the example I shared about the three employees and their supervisor. Each of them had such different reactions to the same words from their supervisor. Their comments reflected their perceptions.

sneaky unreasonable assumptions

Another thing to look out for as you're working with changing this outdated wiring is faulty or unreasonable assumptions masquerading as "the truth."

We've talked about this before and in my experience with clients it helps to be reminded more than once. These assumptions have usually fired up so often that you may not notice them—because they will *feel* true. So, it's going to be important to know what to look for and to watch out for them.

Because these assumptions are most often wired in childhood or times of high stress, they are very concrete and lack the discernment which is possible when the thinking brain is onboard. This means that the assumptions will be "all encompassing," such as "no one appreciates what I do." They also often include the words, "always" and "never."

Let's look at another example. Let's say, a child doesn't get invited to a birthday party. It is easy for them to decide they aren't likable. Children need the thinking brain of an adult to help them understand that not getting invited to a party doesn't mean they aren't likable. All it means is that they didn't get invited.

As adults, when these old assumptions light up you will have the same childlike thoughts and emotions you did when the assumption was formed. You don't get invited, and you feel like it is about you. I was sharing this example with a client, and before I finished, she said, *"I still do that."*

a big matching system

We are all vulnerable to the assumptions wired in our brains because the brain is like a big matching system—constantly trying to match what is happening in the present with something we have experienced in the past to help us deal with the present situation.

So, without you realizing it, your brain can match a situation to an old assumption made in childhood. The assumption may lack any foundation in truth, and in that moment it can "feel" absolutely true. This is what I meant by sneaky unreasonable assumptions.

Let's go back to Beth for a moment.

After working in therapy, Beth knew that her mother cared about her, and she also recognized that they were very different. Yet, when her mother asked, *"Why don't you get your hair styled? Maybe it would help you meet someone,"* all of Beth's logic and understanding were gone.

She came in for a session saying, *"I can't talk with her anymore. She is impossible."*

It took a while for Beth to recognize that her wire of "not being good enough" had been triggered. Beth's emotional brain had matched her mother's comments with a fear wire about "not being good enough," and she was ready to flee. Remember Beth's pattern was to disconnect, and this was what she was ready to do when she heard those words. She no longer wanted to talk with her mother.

Just like Beth's brain did with her mother's comments, your emotional brain is going to be instantaneously matching information from the environment with old experiences and assumptions.

In this intimacy style, keeping others happy is wired with safety, and safety is very important to the brain. It is the brain's primary concern. Because of this, your brain is going to be constantly scanning the environment for signs that someone is unhappy with you. When that matching happens, you are going to find yourself reacting based on old assumptions. For instance, the woman I mentioned a moment ago who said, *"I still do that,"* continued and said, *"When I don't get invited, I decide they really weren't my friend after all."*

Do you see the assumption in there? Not getting invited equals not being her friend. And if we took it further, I imagine that not being her friend meant something about her worth or how lovable she is. As you can imagine, this assumption caused difficulties in her relationships.

It can be tricky to notice when the old unreasonable assumptions of this intimacy style are operating because of how true they feel in the moment. To help with identifying something that feels true and actually isn't, write down what you are feeling and believing, and then read it aloud.

Reading and listening can help you observe and think, which often brings in a new perspective because it uses different parts of the brain. You might also ask yourself, "What would I say if it were a friend telling me this?" Or "Does believing this advocate for or frighten the young part of me or the part who feels my feelings?"

Practicing loving self-compassion as well as the other tools I have shared to calm the nervous system, will also help you think and take perspective.

if you start feeling discouraged

Here are a few other suggestions if you hit a bump in your work on separating your worth from the approval of others.

Remind yourself that you are not alone, and this pull is not a defect in you.

The components of this intimacy style, such as your intuition, caring, and sensitivity to the needs of others are gifts to the world. Because of these qualities, people like you and want to be around you.

When you turn this caring around toward yourself, you are going to be in such luck. How wonderful it will be to have such a kind and caring person, so good at intuiting needs, right there with you for the rest of your life!

So, as you work on bringing your needs into the equation, remember that there are also many good qualities and advantages that you have as a result of learning this style of relating.

And sometimes, just as Beth did, it is helpful to reach out for support.

sometimes two brains are better than one

Just as kids need the thinking brain of an adult to help them calm down, sometimes we adults need another brain to help us catch a faulty assumption.

We are just too deep in the forest to see the trees. If you find yourself in this situation, getting some outside perspective may be just what you need. In doing that, be sure that the perspective is a neutral one. It may be most helpful to find a therapist in your area to work through outdated unreasonable assumptions.

in a nutshell

- It's natural to experience bumps when learning new skills—especially when we are working on changing our core way of relating to others.

- Since connection is wired with safety, intimacy wires will be sturdy wires, and there will be fear and possibly resistance as you work on them. Have compassion for yourself when the road to change is bumpy!

- Keep coming back to yourself with loving self-acceptance, no matter what is happening or what you are noticing.

- The more compassion and love you feel for yourself, and the more you advocate for the part of you who holds your feelings, the more connection you will feel with your own strength and wisdom.

- Sometimes old faulty assumptions are difficult to notice as they "feel" so right or normal.

- Saying them out loud or writing them down and reading them may help you to decide whether the assumptions are factual.

- You might also think about what you would say if a friend made the statement to you. Would you believe it represents the facts?

ideas for reflection

- What bumps do you expect to encounter as you work on separating your worth from the approval of others?
- How will you encourage yourself to keep practicing?
- What support might you need?

chapter eighteen
changes my clients have experienced

I share the following examples of changes my clients have made as examples of possibility. Each of my client's journey has been unique to them, and likewise, your journey will be unique to you. Not all of my clients followed paths similar to those I will share with you. I wouldn't have expected that. And hopefully, these examples will give you some ideas of what might be possible as you work on changing the wires of the entangled intimacy style and separating your worth from the approval of others.

Let's start with Sally.

Sally

Sally was in a new relationship and was struggling with anxiety. As she untangled these intimacy wires, she realized that she was giving all her power to the relationship and the man she was dating.

She realized her anxiety stemmed from feeling powerless to control whether he would choose to stay in the relationship or not.

Sally's safety had been resting in his hands. Whether she was going to be okay depended on whether he continued to "choose her." As long as her safety was in his hands, she felt vulnerable. He had all the power. This seems so obvious reading it, doesn't it? And, in the midst of it, rarely does it feel so clear.

Most times we aren't aware of how approval or acceptance is connected at a deep level with safety—all we feel is worry or fear. For Sally, as long as he was choosing her, she felt safe. And, that safety wasn't very secure, as she had no guarantee that he would stay with her.

I'm starting with Sally because looking for safety outside yourself is at the core of this intimacy style. This pattern can leave you feeling anxious or vulnerable with no real awareness of the source of the vulnerability. This was the case for Sally.

Initially, she was unaware of the true source of her anxiety. Through her work on this intimacy style and her connection with her self, Sally began to "own" who she was in the world and that she was the one who keeps herself safe. This wasn't an overnight change.

Over time, Sally realized she was a strong and intelligent woman, and she had good people skills. She formed relationships easily, and she had many wonderful qualities that she brought to the table in a relationship. When she started focusing on these strengths, her anxiety subsided, and she no longer worried about the relationship ending.

Sally knew that if the relationship didn't work out, she would be okay. She would be sad, and she would be okay. She would be lonely, and she would be okay. Remember the "both/and?" Her work is a great example of connecting with the "both/and."

This didn't mean that Sally didn't need other people or support. We all need connection. What it did was free her up to be herself in the relationship and to think about whether this man was a good match for her.

When her entangled intimacy wires were running the show, all she could think about was keeping him happy and not losing him. Deep down, a similar struggle was raging within Margaret.

Margaret

Margaret really struggled during our work to separate herself from the feelings of the people she loved. She had a hard time in the beginning even imagining putting her needs before those of her husband.

Just to be clear, there are certainly times we put other's needs ahead of our own. This is part of the give and take of a relationship. And if you are continually putting other people's needs ahead of your own, especially without checking in with yourself first, there will be consequences.

In Margaret's case, when she thought about bringing her needs back into the picture, especially if it meant putting her needs before those of her husband's or disagreeing with him, strong fears of abandonment came up. Margaret knew that her fears weren't rational. She didn't believe her husband would leave her.

And the fear was there. A deep, primitive fear of abandonment.

The better Margaret got at comforting herself and bringing herself back into balance when those fears came up, the more connected she was with the facts of the situation; her husband wouldn't abandon her if she took steps to care for herself and if the worst case happened and he did, she would deal with it. Dealing with the fear allowed her to bring her needs into the picture.

And remember how Margaret was working on noticing her feelings at the same time that she noticed how her husband was feeling? Doing this had a big impact on her ability to pay attention to her feelings. She discovered that although they often felt differently, nothing had changed in their relationship. As a result, she started to feel secure that she had a right to her feelings and that she wouldn't be abandoned when she felt them.

In fact, Margaret was surprised by the impact her self-care had on her marriage. When she started identifying her feelings and needs and being direct in her communication, a funny and unexpected thing happened: her husband became more attentive. It was exactly the opposite of what Margaret had been expecting and fearing.

It turned out that Margaret's husband had been reacting to her appeasing and also to her hinting at what she wanted him to do without directly asking him. His first wife had done this with him, and as a result, it was a "hot button" for him. He pulled away when Margaret hinted at what she needed rather than asking directly.

Margaret's interpretation of him pulling away was that it wasn't okay for her to ask for what she needed. In truth, she wasn't really asking; she was hoping he would intuit what she needed in true entangled style.

When Margaret started asking more directly for what she wanted and needed from him, he responded in a much more positive way. She more often got what she needed from the relationship. She felt more cared for and heard. And Margaret didn't spend her time feeling responsible for her husband's feelings or the mess her teenagers made and how it might cause him stress. It took time, and Margaret started to "get" that he was responsible for his feelings, not her.

Beth

Remember Beth, who struggled with her mother because of their many differences? Beth didn't want to change her appearance in the way her mother hoped she would, nor could she share her mother's political views. She felt trapped because her wiring led her to believe that to love her mother, she needed to keep her mother happy.

In working on this intimacy style, Beth continued to struggle with her mother. There was just so much history there. And her ability to hold on to herself in the midst of her mother's disapproval became much stronger.

Beth began to understand and feel compassion for her mother's perspectives. She began to experience more and more moments with her mother when she could hold on to a new understanding; that, even though they disagreed, they could love each other and be in relationship. And most importantly, that even though they disagreed, she was a good and lovable person.

In the meantime, Beth really tapped into who she was and what was important to her. She became expressive of her style of being in the world, even though it differed from her mother's. She also rarely turned to food in the way she had before.

Madeline

Madeline, the supervisor who often ended up doing her employees' work, because she lost track of her own needs when she felt her employees' pain, came up with a phrase to help herself with this tendency. She would stop and regularly ask herself, *"How full is my tank?"*

This helped Madeline stay aware of her needs when her employees were struggling and it also gave her time to decide on how to respond to requests in her personal life. It helped her consider her needs before automatically agreeing to help.

Many women have found Madeline's question to be a good one. Others have used the question, *"How much is in my bank account?"* And, *"Can I afford to make another withdrawal?"*

Either of these questions might help you to check in with how much you have to give before saying "yes" to a request.

Karen

Karen, the happily married woman who realized that she had stopped being herself once she married, reconnected with her interests and passions. She created a space in her house that was hers alone, where she could sew and work on her crafts.

Karen had been fearful of sharing her feelings and opinions with her family based on her early experiences in her family of origin. Like Margaret, she was pleasantly surprised.

Karen found that her opinions were welcomed, and no one in her family seemed to mind or notice that she was taking time for herself.

She said:

"I feel free in a way that I haven't felt in years."

Olivia

Olivia was embarrassed to do the outdoor activities she loved in the world for fear of being judged by her weight.

With time, she started chipping away at those old wires that equated her size with her worth. Olivia became an advocate for the idea that athletes come in all sizes. She now supports other women in accepting themselves and their bodies.

One of Olivia's struggles with being a large woman had been that she couldn't find athletic clothing that fit her. In the beginning, every time she put on her athletic clothes, and they were tight, she fell into shame.

At some point, she realized this situation was ridiculous. She was a strong athletic woman who deserved to have clothes that fit and were comfortable.

She contacted a company where she shopped and expressed her concerns about the lack of clothing to fit athletic women in large bodies. To her surprise and joy, they started carrying larger sizes.

it isn't easy, and who knows what is possible

The work may not be easy, and the possibilities are greater than what you might imagine. I hope these examples have helped you realize this.

None of these women could have imagined where they would be

after working on the patterns related to the entangled intimacy style.

This is not to say that those old wires never light up for these women. I'm imagining they do. And they are now in a much better place to deal with them and give themselves the care they need.

Replacing those old beliefs with new empowering beliefs such as:

- I am valuable, even if you don't see it.
- I am valuable, even if you disagree.
- You can disagree and not like what I am doing, and I know I am still okay.
- I can choose whether I want to have a relationship with you.
- It is not my job to make you like me because I know that I have value either way.

you can do it

You may not believe those statements right now, and that's okay. The woman whose stories I just shared with you didn't believe it in the beginning, either.

It is hard to believe we can do something when we first start to do it, isn't it? I was recently getting back into yoga and was shocked and frustrated with my lack of balance. My thoughts went something like this, *"What the heck? I will never be able to do this!"* A few weeks later, I was surprised to notice that I was holding that pose with ease. I never would have imagined it was possible that first day.

Can you think of an example like this in your own life? Something you never thought you could do and then later discovered you were doing with ease?

No matter what your path is like learning these skills, be kind to yourself. Your journey is your journey. See if you can celebrate the journey and let go of expectations for how it will end or what it looks like.

If you are comparing yourself to the stories of the women in this book, your entangled intimacy wires are likely firing up. This is natural and a risk of reading a book like this for anyone who has an entangled intimacy style. This is an opportunity to bring new information into those old wires pushing you to compare yourself with others.

The changes these women made were the changes that were right for them. Your path may be very different. Remember the rose and the orchid. Both are beautiful, and one cannot be the other. Use the concept of your entelechy or that God or the universe has a plan for you to support you as you travel down a path that is yours alone—one that is not for me or anyone else to determine.

And as you do that, do your best to keep both wheels of the "cart" turning.

in a nutshell

- In this chapter, I have shared some of the changes that my clients made in working on separating their worth from the approval of others.

- Not every client made the types of changes described in this chapter, and I wouldn't have expected that.

- I share my clients' experiences to give you hope and a sense of what might be possible by doing the work of the BLOOM model.

- Although there were similarities in my clients' journey's, their journeys were unique to them, as yours will be to you.

- Remember the rose and the orchid. Both are beautiful, and one can't be the other.

- If you find yourself comparing yourself to the women I describe in this chapter, it is likely that the wires of your entangled intimacy style have fired up.

- This is an opportunity to remind yourself of your entelechy or that God or the universe has a plan for you and to bring new information into those old wires leading you to make comparisons.

- No matter what your path is like learning these skills, be kind to yourself. Your journey is your journey. See if you can celebrate the journey and let go of expectations for how it will end or what it looks like.

- Sending love and support for your blossoming in whatever form that takes!

ideas for reflection

- What feelings came up for you as you read these women's stories?
- Did you notice any old wires of comparison coming up?
- If so, take a moment to feel compassion for yourself. It is natural that these wires would light up. This is a moment of opportunity to bring some new information into these wires. See if you can identify the core unreasonable assumptions. What new information needs to come into these wires?

chapter nineteen
thoughts as I leave you

Change is hard no matter what we are trying to change. When it comes to changing our basic style of relating with others, well, that's a challenge.

And change is possible, as I have just shared with you. We know that our brain continues to change throughout our lives and that what we do, think, feel, and imagine affects the structure of the brain. With enough repetition, our brain makes it easier for us. And in the beginning, we need to be purposeful and mindful of our thoughts and actions.

An easy way to imagine this process is to imagine the task of creating a new trail in the forest. Similar to other areas of our lives where we gravitate toward doing things the way we always have done them—when hiking people are drawn to an existing trail if one is available. You can also see this happening when people cut across a lawn; they tend to use the same path others have used to cross the lawn.

Thinking about our pull to existing trails or paths is an easy way of picturing the brain's pull to well-used pathways—the defaults. If you want to create change in a default pathway, it's a bit like creating a new trail in the forest. Clearing a new path in the forest isn't easy. There are things to trip over. Branches are hitting you in the face. If there is a path nearby, even a deer trail, you will feel pulled toward using it, despite your goal of creating a new trail. And what happens after you have gone down that new trail 10 times, 50 times, 100 times? It gets easier, right? And each time, because it is easier, you feel rewarded and want to keep going, making it an even easier trail to use. By the hundredth time, maybe even the fiftieth, you can easily talk and walk at the same time.

Creating a new trail in the forest is similar to the process of creating new pathways in your brain. When you first do something new, it is difficult. It will not feel natural. You have to pay attention and you will likely feel a pull to go back to the old way of doing things. And what happens after you have done it for a while? It gets easier, doesn't it? And, if you do it long enough, what happens?

It becomes the new normal, right?

I share this with you because your work on changing the patterns of the entangled intimacy style will most likely take a similar course. It will likely feel exciting in the beginning, and then more challenging as you work on changing old patterns.

If you get discouraged with your progress, remember the analogy of creating a hiking trail. Or, if you don't hike, you might picture rain on a hillside that has no grass or vegetation to stop the water's flow. At first, the rain will run down every which way and before long, channels will form, and the water will follow them.

Likewise, at first it may feel like you are a bit "all over the place" as you look at these patterns and work on changing them. And with time and persistence, I bet you will see the difference you are making.

small changes—big effects

Or, as Rick Hanson Ph.D. so beautifully described it in his book *Buddha's Brain,*

> *"A single raindrop doesn't have much effect, but if you have enough raindrops and enough time, you can carve a Grand Canyon."* [74]

He goes on to say, *"To keep at it, you need to be on your own side."*

Isn't that really what we have been talking about and working on in this book? You, being on your side? As you work to create new pathways in your life and in your brain, remember to be on your side and to be kind to yourself.

No matter where you are in the process of separating your worth from the approval of others, practice loving acceptance and compassion. You are where you are, and it takes as long as it takes. Of all the steps in the BLOOM model, loving acceptance and self-compassion are the most important. Giving yourself the gift of that kind of caring, alone, can make a difference in your life. Feeling acceptance and compassion can calm your nervous system and feeling them can also help to lessen the emotional "punch" of a memory.

We can bring new emotions into old memories by the way we feel about them, as we remember them. This is why siblings who shared the same experience often recall it in different ways, especially with the passing of time.

Feeling compassion and loving acceptance as you recall painful memories or difficult situations adds those feelings to the memory—feelings that may not have been possible or available when the memory was initially formed. In thinking about that, it seems we have the potential to rewrite our histories.

And, most importantly, knowing that you will be there for yourself in a loving way, no matter what, is powerful. There can be a safety there, which just isn't possible when you look to others to be sure you are "okay."

my hopes for you

As you come to the end of this book, I hope you realize that there is nothing wrong with you if you have been measuring your worth by the approval of others. Of course, you would seek approval. Our history as women, our socialization and big industries ensure that we look outside of ourselves for our value.

My greatest hope is for you to know you are wonderful, just as you are right now. There is nothing "wrong" with you. I bet you are a loving, giving, capable, intuitive woman.

And I hope as you read this book, you have checked out whether the strong force of an entangled intimacy style has been pulling you to give beyond your ability to give—past your limits and your resources and to measure your worth by other's approval of you and what you do.

If that force is alive and well within you, I hope reading about it has helped you understand the strong emotional pull you feel to keep other people happy. That many of the symptoms you have been experiencing such as exhaustion, anxiety, anger, resentment, rage, depression, overeating, drinking, or overspending are very likely symptoms of this pattern and not problems in and of themselves that you need to solve.

I hope you feel relieved knowing that pull you feel to seek approval isn't about a defect in you and instead is simply outdated or defective default wiring—wiring which most likely reflects the experience of your female ancestors or quite possibly fear that lives in the collective female consciousness.

My larger hope is that the BLOOM model has helped you "light a candle" of loving self-acceptance and compassion for yourself.

And that as you have brought your attention back to yourself, you have discovered a treasure chest inside that has been just waiting for you to tap into it. A treasure chest filled with wisdom, strength, and power, as well as a roadmap that is yours alone.

And as you continue to connect with yourself, I hope that connection will open you up to the support of those around you, as well as larger sources of support like the spiritual—in whatever way you define it—and the universe. I trust that all the energy of the universe will be there, ready to support you as you move toward becoming all that you can and were meant to be.

As each woman connects with her inner knowing and feels supported in doing so, I imagine a shift in the female collective consciousness as well as in the patterns we as women pass to the women who follow us.

My hope is that as we do this, a new norm will be established—a norm in which women have separated their worth from the approval of others and in which women support each other in all of our uniqueness.

And by doing this, I hope we will create a world where women are supported in sharing their voices and their female perspectives.

Because we need more women's voices.

Let's start with yours!

in a nutshell

- Change is hard no matter what it is we are trying to change, and when we are trying to change our core style of relating with others it can be a challenge.

- And small changes over time turn into big changes. The more you practice with the skills, the more your brain will create the structure to make those skills more natural in the future.

- No matter where you are in the process of separating your worth from the approval of others be kind and accepting of yourself.

- Of all the steps in the model, loving self-compassion, and acceptance are most important. It is okay to be right where you are in this process. Where you are today means nothing about where you will be tomorrow.

- I hope that as we each work on this connection between our worth and approval that we create a world in which all women feel safe to be themselves and in which we each support each other in all of our uniqueness.

ideas for reflection

- What thoughts and emotions are coming up as you finish this book?

- What are you feeling inspired to do?

- What small change might you make that over time might grow into a well-traveled highway?

- How might your work on being yourself in the world inspire or support other women in being themselves in the world?

are you feeling inspired?

Education is not the filling of a pail,
but the lighting of a fire."

- William Butler Yeats

will you help spread the light of self-acceptance?

If you feel inspired by what you have learned in this book, will you help spread the light by leaving a positive review wherever you purchased this book?

Without positive reviews and sales, few, if any, women will see and have the chance to read this book because reviews determine whether a book will be seen and purchased. So please take a moment and help future readers decide to buy this book.

You may imagine that your review won't make a difference and I want to be sure you know that it will. Every positive review of the book will increase the probability of other women benefitting from it. **Your voice matters!**

Your review doesn't need to be eloquent or lengthy — simple share your heart-felt reactions and/or how the book made a difference in your life.

Please help me reach more women.
We need your voice to do that!

And if, in addition to your review, you have comments or feedback that you would like to share with me personally, I would love to hear from you. The best way to do that is to send me an email at info@creatingchoicesdeblang.com. I learn so much from the feedback I receive and so I look forward to hearing from you.

Before you go....

where to go from here

I hope reading this book has been lighting a fire within you! And if you are like me, you often feel inspired by a book, have great intentions to apply what you have read, and then later find the book forgotten under a pile of other things. It's frustrating, isn't it? Or maybe, instead, you've been trying to practice with the skills, and they are nowhere to be found when you need them.

For most people, skills make sense when reading them, and are harder to apply in real life. Both forgetting about new intentions and remembering to use new skills reflect your brain's preference for efficiency and attempts to predict what will be helpful in the present based on what you did in the past. Why take a road just being built when you could take a highway?

The good news is that whatever you do, think, feel, or imagine with enough frequency, the brain creates the structure to support it, making it easier and more natural in the future. In this way, new roads in the brain turn into highways with enough use. And with enough exposure and practice, new skills can become the highway of choice. I've seen what can happen when women give themselves the support they need to start trusting their own wisdom, and I want that for you.

What do you suppose is the support you need to make that happen? Will reading the book be enough? Or would it help to have more input from me to ensure that you can call up the skills when you need them? Or do you need the support of working with an individual therapist in your area?

If it is continued input you need, I want to offer that to you through the online companion course for this book. In the course, you will have the opportunity to gain more exposure to the skills and information you have just learned in *Never Enough* so that your brain will begin to support you rather than work against you in feeling "enough" and in separating your worth from what others think of you.

Just imagine how it will feel knowing how to calm yourself and go on with your day after someone is disapproving of you. Or imagine knowing how to connect with your own wisdom and strength and beginning to trust yourself. And imagine how you will feel if you don't give yourself the support you need.

If these skills are new to you or you are having trouble applying them, please don't be hard on yourself. More exposure may be just what you need. One way of getting that exposure is through the online companion course for this book. I invite you to check out here: Bit.ly/neverenoughonline

I hope you will take the time to decide what will be most helpful in getting you to the place where you can say with conviction,

"I deserve to be me, even if you disagree!"

with much warmth and caring,

Deb

P.S. Who might you help "light a candle" of loving self-acceptance and compassion in their life by telling them about this book and course?

acknowledgments

How can I possibly acknowledge all the people who helped me get to the place of writing and publishing this book? I can't. It would be another book. So, if you don't see your name here, please know it is not for a lack of appreciation and instead reflects my trying to put feelings larger than words into words.

First and foremost, I want to thank all the women who shared with me their struggles with an entangled intimacy style and the strong pull they felt to appease and gain approval. It takes real guts to bare your soul in therapy. I admire and have learned from each one of you. I feel honored to have been a part of your journeys. And without your willingness to share, I wouldn't have noticed this pattern, and this book wouldn't be a reality.

I feel grateful to my mentors, coaches, and therapists who have encouraged me to trust myself and to know that it is okay to be where I am, even if it's not where I think I "should" be.

Stepping back in time, I feel grateful to my professors for helping me realize the power of really listening. Without this skill, I wouldn't have noticed this common thread underneath so many of the struggles that were bringing women through my door.

I especially want to acknowledge Judy Zehr, LPC, a gifted therapist with a love of science, who took the time to review the book for me. Much gratitude as well, Judy, for your caring and inspiring guidance as I looked at my own outdated, unreasonable assumptions through my personal work.

Tracy Fairbanks, M.D., thank you for taking time from your busy medical practice to read this book and Laura Edwards-Leeper, Ph.D., for jumping in and recruiting a cohort of friends and colleagues when I was stuck on a decision and for doing some spur of the moment content review for me. Thank you both for being there when I needed help.

I want to thank Corey Clark for rooting for me along the way, my sister, Hallie Erbacher, for encouraging me to get back on track after a knee replacement derailed me, and my niece, Jacqueline Erbacher for her input on my cover designs. I also want to express my gratitude to my current clients whose excitement about the book was contagious and a wonderful incentive to get it finished and into the hands of my readers.

Angela E. Lauria, Ph.D., thank you for inspiring me to consider the difference I was meant to make in the world, to believe that I could write a book, and for providing a structure that helped me start putting words that have been living in my head for such a long time on to paper.

What a wonderful choice I made in choosing The Sage Proofreader, Susan Michaud to edit my book. Your calming, encouraging presence was such a gift—just the balm I needed. And of course, there was the huge relief knowing you were there with me, checking my words, and offering suggestions and feedback. Thank you for standing by me and supporting me throughout this process. It is hard to put into words how much gratitude I feel for you being "in my corner" in this endeavor!

Many thanks to the team at Self-Publishing School for all the ways that each of you contributed to helping this book become a reality. I want to especially thank Ellaine Kiel for your guidance, kindness, enthusiasm, and continued support and encouragement. Kerk Murray thank you for your patience and understanding during my last push to the finish line.

My thanks to Jamie from Audio Creation Services for being so patient and kind in waiting for files and reworking them as you edited and created the audio version of my book. You did a fantastic job and I feel so grateful for your help in making my audio book a reality.

Oh, how blessed I was to have found Books to Hook Publishing to make my book available to my readers. I am amazed by all of the ways you jumped in to fix what needed to be fixed and do what needed to be done. Your prompt and efficient attention as well as your experience and support were such amazing gifts after this long bumpy journey. It is hard for me to capture the depth of my gratitude in words. Thank you!

And finally, thanks to Lakshman. N., for my wonderful cover. What would a book be without a cover to entice women to pick it up? Thank you for helping me make that a reality.

notes

1. Begley, S. (2007). <u>Train your mind: Change your Brain. How a new science reveals our extraordinary potential to transform ourselves.</u> New York: Ballantine Books.

2. Pipher, M. (1994). <u>Reviving Ophelia: Saving the selves of adolescent girls.</u> New York: Ballantine Books.

3. Beattie, M. (1987). <u>Codependent no more.</u> San Francisco: Hazelden Foundation.

4. Gibson, L. C. (2015). <u>Adult children of emotionally immature parents.</u> Oakland: New Harbinger.

5. Church, D. (2015). <u>The genie in your genes: Epigenetic medicine and the new biology of intention.</u> Energy Psychology Press.

6. Church, D. (2021, February 16). *Krugerrands, King George III and tapping!* [Newsletter] Retrieved from https://eftuniverse.ontraport.com.

7. Holland, J. (2006). <u>A brief history of misogyny: the world's oldest prejudice.</u> London: Little Brown Book Group.

8. New York Historical Society. (2018) *Teaching Women's History: The Marginalization of Women.* Retrieved from https://www.nyhistory.org/blogs/teaching-womens-history-marginalization-of-women.

9. National Archives. (2022). *19th Amendment to the U.S. Constitution: Women's Right to Vote (1920)*. Retrieved from www.archives.gov>milestones>19thamendment

10. Sullivan, M. (2021, March 14). Online harassment of female journalists is real, and it's increasingly hard to endure. The Washington Post. Retrieved from: https://www.washingtonpost.com/lifestyle/media/online-harassment-female-journalists/2021/03/13/ed24b0aa-82aa-11eb-ac37-4383f7709abe_story.html

11. Sullivan, M. (2021, March 14). Online harassment of female journalists is real, and it's increasingly hard to endure. The Washington Post. Retrieved from: https://www.washingtonpost.com/lifestyle/media/online-harassment-female-journalists/2021/03/13/ed24b0aa-82aa-11eb-ac37-4383f7709abe_story.html

12. Hesse, M. (2021, February 11). Capitol rioters searched for Nancy Pelosi in a way that should make everyone's skin crawl. The Washington Post. Retrieved from https://www.reddit.com/r/politics/comments/lhg17i/capitol_rioters_searched_for_nancy_pelosi_in_a/?utm_source=BD&utm_medium=Search&utm_name=Bing&utm_content=PSR3

13. Carter, C.M. (2022) Retrieved from https://christinemichelcarter.com

14. Keller, R. (n.d.) *Why Women Need to Climb Mountains—on a Journey through the Life and Vision of Dr. Gerda Lerner.* A

documentary retrieved from Womenneedtoclimbmountains.
com

15. Pipher, M. (1994). <u>Reviving Ophelia: Saving the elves of adolescent girls.</u> New York: Ballantine Books p 20.

16. Kessler-Harris, A. (n.d.) *Women Have Always Worked.* Columbia University online XSeries Program. Retrieved from courses.edx.org

17. Berger, J. (1990). <u>Ways of seeing.</u> London: British Broadcasting Corporation and Penguin Books.

18. Orbach, S. (1978). <u>Fat is a feminist issue</u>. London: Penguin Random House.

19. Hirschmann, J.R. & Munter, C. H. (1995). <u>When women stop hating their bodies; Freeing yourself from food and weight obsession.</u> New York: Ballantine Publishing Group. p 13

20. Wolf, N. (2002). <u>The beauty myth; How images of beauty are used against women.</u> New York: HarperCollins.

21. Baker, J. (2015). <u>Things no one will tell fat girls.</u> Berkeley: Seal Press.

22. Further research has been conducted since these books were published and they will give you a good starting place. Campos, P. (2004). <u>The obesity myth; Why America's obsession with weight is hazardous to your health.</u> New York: Penguin Group.

23. Bacon, L. (2008). Health at every size; <u>The surprising truth about</u>

your weight and your health. Dallas: BenBella Books, Inc.

24. Gaesser, G.A. (2002). The truth about your weight and health. Carlsbad: Gürze Books.

25. Here is one example of the studies suggesting an obesity paradox. Smith, M.J. (2020). Obesity paradox: Outcomes better in heavier emergency surgery patients. General Surgery News. Retrieved from https://www.generalsurgerynews.com/In-the-News/Article/07-20/Obesity-Paradox-Outcomes-Better-in-Heavier-Emergency-Surgery-Patients/58954

26. Again, here is one example. Matheson, E. M., King, D.E. & Everett, C. J. (2012, Jan-Feb). Health lifestyle habits and mortality in overweight and obese individuals. J Am Board Fam Med. doi: 10.3122/jabfm.2012.01.110164.

27. Vadiveloo, M. & Mattei, J. (2017). Perceived weight discrimination and 10-year risk of allostatic load among US adults. Journal of the American Board of Family Medicine. 25, 9-12.

28. The U.S. weight loss & diet control Market (2021-March). Retrieved from http://www.researchandmarkets.com

29. Strings, S. (2019). Fearing the Black body; The racial origins of fat phobia. New York: University Press

30. Wolf, N. (1984). The beauty myth; How images of beauty are used against women. New York: Harper Collins. p 10.

31. Chernin, K. (1982). <u>The obsession: Reflections on the tyranny of slenderness.</u> New York: Harper & Row. p 3.

32. Orbach, S. (1978). <u>Fat is a feminist issue. London:</u> Penguin Random House.

33. Paige, L. Lolita, Twiggy, patriarchy, *Oh, my! 1960's fashion & the waves of feminism.* Thevintagewomanmagazine.com. Retrieved from https://thevintagewomanmagazine.com/lolita-twiggy-patriarchy-oh-my-1960s-fashion-the-waves-of-feminism

34. Wolf, N. (1991). <u>The beauty myth; how images of beauty are used against women.</u> New York: HarperCollins. p 184.

35. Strings, S. (2019). <u>Fearing the Black body; The racial origins of fat phobia.</u> New York: University Press.

36. Sole-Smith, V. (2021, March 6). <u>In obesity research, fatphobia is always the X factor. Scientific American.</u> Retrieved from https://www.scientificamerican.com/article/in-obesity-research-fatphobia-is-always-the-x-factor

37. Aamodt, S. (2016). <u>Why diets make us fat.</u> New York: Penguin Random House.

38. Mann, T. (2015). <u>Secrets from the eating lab.</u> New York: Harper Collins.

39. Matz, J. & Frankel, E. (2014). <u>Beyond a shadow of a diet. The comprehensive guide to treating binge eating disorder, Compulsive eating, and emotional overeating.</u> Second Edition.

New York: Routledge.

40. Blake, C.E., Hébert J.R., Lee, D.C., Adams, S.A., Steck, S.E., Sui,X., Kuk, J.L., Baruth, M., & Blair, S.N. (2013). Adults with greater weight satisfaction report more positive health behaviors and have better health status regardless of BMI. Journal of Obesity. http://www.ncbi.nlm.nih.gov/pmc/articles/PMC3686087/

41. Wirth, M.D., Blake, C.E, Hébert, J.R., Sux, X, & Blair, S.N. (2014). Chronic weight dissatisfaction predicts Type 2 diabetes risk: Aerobic Center longitudinal study. Health Psychology. 33(8), 912-919.

42. Begley, S. (2007). Train your mind: Change your Brain. How a new science reveals our extraordinary potential to transform ourselves. New York: Ballantine Books.

43. Hawkins, D.R. (2002). Power vs force; The hidden determinants of human behavior. United States: Hay House.

44. Kerr, M.E. & Bowen, M. (1988). Family evaluation. New York & London: W.W. Norton & Company.

45. Mellin, L. (2010). Wired for joy; A revolutionary method for creating happiness from within. United States: Hay House.

46. Merriam-Webster. Online reference. Retrieved from https://www.merriam-webster.com/

47. Gentry, E.J. (2016). Forward facing trauma; Healing the moral

wound. Sarasota: Compassion Unlimited. (2011). Mindsight. The New Science of Personal Transformation. New York: Bantam Books.

48. Siegel Daniel J. (2011). <u>Mindsight</u>. The new science of personal transformation. New York: Bantam Books

49. Houston J. *Awakening to your life's purpose.* Online course through Evolving Wisdom. Retrieved from https://www. evolvingwisdom.com

50. Houston J. (2014, January 7) Facebook post. Retrieved from https://www.facebook.com/jean.houston.page/ posts/583441185065353

51. Houston, J.(Online course) *Awakening to your life's purpose. through Evolving Wisdom.* Retrieved from https://www. evolvingwisdom.com

52. Houston, J. (Online course) *Awakening to your life's purpose. through Evolving Wisdom.* Retrieved from https://www. evolvingwisdom.com

53. Ranganathan, V.K., Siemionow, V., Liu, J.Z., Sahgal, V.& Yue, G.H. (2004). From mental power to muscle power—gaining strength by using the mind. <u>Neuropsychologia</u>. 42(7):944-56.

54. Church, D. (2015). <u>The genie in your genes: Epigenetic medicine and the new biology of intention.</u> Energy Psychology Press.

55. Crum, A., Corbin, W.R., Brownwell, K.D., & Salovey, P. (2011).

Mind over milkshakes: Mindsets, not just nutrients, determine ghrelin response. <u>Health Psychology</u> 30(4): 424-9.

56. McTaggart, L. <u>The intention experiement: using your thoughts to change your life and the world.</u> New York: Atria

57. Dispenza, J. (2012). <u>Breaking the habit of being yourself.</u> Hay House.

58. Wood, W. (2019). <u>Good habits, bad habits; The science of making positive changes that stick.</u> New York: Farrar, Straus and Giroux.

59. Dispenza, J. (2012). <u>Breaking the habit of being yourself: How to lose your mind and create a new one.</u> USA: Hay House.

60. Neff, K. (2011). <u>Self-compassion; Stop beating yourself up and leave insecurity behind.</u> New York: HarperCollins.

61. McGonigal, K. (2021). (Online Course). *Three tools to help a client reverse a sense of worthlessness.* In: Working with core beliefs of 'never enough.' Retrieved from https://www.nicabm.com/

62. Salzberg, S. (2002). <u>Loving kindness; the revolutionary art of happiness.</u> Boston & London: Shambhala.

63. Ogden, P. (2021). (Online Course). *A bottom-up approach to work with implicit memories of inadequacy.* In: Working with core beliefs of 'never enough.' Retrieved from https://www.nicabm.com/

64. Church, D., Yount, G., & Brooks, A.J. (2010). The effects of emotional freedom techniques on stress biochemistry: a

randomized controlled trial. <u>Journal of Nervous and Mental Disease.</u> 200(10), 891-896.

65. A good place to start in learning about energy psychology is The Association for Comprehensive Energy Psychology. They also offer self-help videos. https://www.energypsych.org/page/Consumers

1. Another good source of information on energy psychology and tapping is EFT Universe. https://www.EFTuniverse.com

2. Rosenberg, M.B. (2015). <u>Nonviolent communication: A language of life</u>. Encinitas C

3. A: PuddleDancer Press.

4. Mellin, L. Communication during group training.

5. Mellin, L. Communication during group training.

6. Mellin, L. Communication during group training.

7. Ecker, B. (2015). Memory reconsolidation understood and misunderstood. <u>International Journal of Neuropsychotherapy.</u> 10, 1-46. DOI: 10.12744/ijnpt.2015.0002-0046.

8. Dispenza, J. (2012). <u>Breaking the habit of being yourself: How to lose your mind and create a new one.</u> USA: Hay House.

9. His Holiness the Dalai Lama, Archbishop Desmond Tutu, with Douglas Abrams. (2016). <u>The book of joy: Lasting happiness in a changing world.</u> New York: Random House.

10. Hanson, R. (2009). <u>Buddha's brain; The practical neuroscience of happiness, love & wisdom.</u> Oakland: New Harbinger Publications, Inc., p 44; p 19.

about the author

Dr. Deb Lang has worked as a Licensed Psychologist in private practice since 1995. Prior to that she worked as a Licensed Professional Counselor and she began her professional career working as a Registered Dietitian. While working as a psychologist she has provided therapy for individuals and groups as well as supervision for other clinicians working toward licensure. Besides work in private practice, she has worked in hospitals, a wellness center and university counseling centers.

Deb's early experiences, as a dietitian, listening to the internalized guilt and shame of women failing to lose weight inspired a life-long journey of helping women accept themselves and celebrate their own beauty and truth. A desire to inspire self-compassion propelled her to become a Licensed Psychologist and now a writer. Deb loves learning and sharing what she learns with others. She especially enjoys sharing knowledge about the brain and body—knowledge that normalize experiences and behaviors. She feels passionate about sharing skills that help women connect with their own internal wisdom. Over the years she has taught numerous classes and workshops for students and the community.

Never Enough is her first published self-help book. She has written a couple more in her mind. If you are an introvert, you will know what she means. Hopefully, those will be available for you to read soon.

Deb lives in the mountains in Montana and when she is not writing or working with clients, she is most often out in nature, hiking, biking or cross-country skiing. When inside she is reading, painting or trying to wrangle all the hair that comes from with living with two large livestock guardian dogs and one very lovable cat.